ANTIQUES and ART
How to Know, Buy and Use Them

ANTIQUES
and ART

*How to Know, Buy
and Use Them*

BY

Howard L. Katzander

INTRODUCTION BY
Peter C. Wilson, *Chairman,*
Sotheby Parke Bernet Group, Ltd.

DOUBLEDAY & COMPANY, Inc.
Garden City, New York

CONTENTS

FOREWORD

THIS BOOK had its genesis some fifteen years ago when I moved into a five-story ten-room house in New York City with the battered remnants of a broken marriage that had been lived out in a four-room apartment. There was an immediate need to furnish a rather stately living room, a library, and a dining room. There was also a desire to furnish well, which was not matched by the resources at hand.

One tour of the antique dealers' establishments on Fifty-seventh Street and Madison Avenue, as well as a look at the less pretentious shops on Third and Second avenues, offered convincing proof that the vast rooms I was confronted with would stay empty a long time if I had to furnish them out of those shops.

So I began going to the auctions.

That was a different story. I very quickly learned that it would be possible with available funds to furnish my home with well-made, well-styled examples of antique furniture that would look, once they were in place, as though they had been there forever. Buying furniture at auction, I found, had one major disadvantage—it was not possible to do the job in one massive buying foray, as one could by using the full facilities of a big furniture store, including their decorators and contract workshops.

There were, however, overriding advantages.

For one, there were no bills, no deferred payments to be made, no interest to be paid. For another, the quality of the furniture available in the retail stores, except for contemporary reproductions which are often of high quality, left much to be desired.

Most important, by buying at auction, piece by piece, it became necessary to furnish slowly, to compose a room as though it were a work of art, which indeed the setting in which we spend so much of our lives should be.

Out of that experience came a professional involvement in the auction market as a writer and reporter, in the course of which the knowledge gained in those early forays into the market has been substantially broadened and confirmed.

This book is designed to bring that broad knowledge to those of limited means and a hunger for beauty in their surroundings that they cannot otherwise satisfy.

Woodbury, New York
June, 1977

INTRODUCTION

by Peter C. Wilson, *Chairman*
Sotheby Parke Bernet Group, Ltd.

MORE AND MORE people when furnishing their houses are buying antiques in the broadest sense—that is to say, furniture and works of art of every kind produced before 1939—because they find that these objects give them personal satisfaction, give character to their rooms and (a relevant consideration to many people) their purchases are likely to increase in value after a few years. They are also not unmindful of the fact that these objects have stood the stresses of life for one or many more generations and will survive far into the future.

The interest in works of art too is more widely spread today than ever before. The number of people visiting museums has vastly increased; millions of people every year visit private collections throughout the world; every week, references are made on television to works of art and often programs are shown concerning museums, exhibitions, artists or the art market. Never before have so many well-illustrated books on works of art been published. All these factors have had a great effect on our appreciation and enjoyment of antiques and art.

When furnishing a room with antiques there is no necessity to restrict oneself to a single style or period. To do so can make the general effect dreary and priggish. It is far safer, and far easier, to buy things you like—pottery or porcelain, oak or mahogany furniture, Victoriana, peasant wares or the most sophisticated objects and jumble them up together to get the effect you want. To mingle amongst these some modern things—glass-topped tables, comfortable sofas and chairs, lamps and so on—improves the atmosphere of the room.

Mr. Katzander skillfully guides us in the way to find and buy antiques. The best advice, he points out, is first and foremost to buy things we really like and not those which are supposed to be most likely to increase in value, and then to seek the counsel from time to time of experienced dealers (especially those the contents of whose shops appeal to you) or of a friend whose taste you admire.

If you are interested in antiques and works of art, generally a journey to almost any city has a reward in store for you. There is the museum to visit and then, with luck, there are antique shops with their promise of the discovery of the very thing you want. If you find it, do not be worried too much by the price—it is better to pay a little more than perhaps you think, rightly or wrongly, it is worth, than to pass it by and settle later for second best. After all it is you who will be living with it for many years to come and once paid for, the cost is forgotten like last year's telephone bills.

Works of art are often not expensive if you relate them to the cost of other things today and they are increasingly coming within the reach of more and more people. Start buying now (if you are not already set on this road) and add a new pleasure to your life— however modest your means.

ANTIQUES and ART
How to Know, Buy and Use Them

CHAPTER
1

ANTIQUES TO FIT YOUR POCKETBOOK

MOST BOOKS on collecting art and antiques are written about the very rich to be read by the not so rich. Their aim is to titillate and to entertain rather than to inform. They consist, on the one hand, of anecdotes about the collecting experiences of the Mellons, the Morgans, the titled gentry of Britain, and those of such latter-day Croesuses as Norton Simon, the West Coast industrialist. These stories set out in contrasting patterns the pitfalls that lie in fakery and lack of knowledge, against a heady tapestry woven of lost "masterpieces" regained in unlikely circumstances and sold for vast sums.

There is no reason to disparage such books. They are entertaining, the stories are often true, the lost "masterpieces" frequently turn out to be real finds.

On the other hand, there are many books devoted to the specialized interests of collectors, covering every conceivable aspect of collecting. They are of value and of interest to everyone seriously interested in learning about art and antiques.

This is a different kind of book—one that is written for *users* of art and antiques rather than for collectors, for home decorators of a very special kind rather than for those looking for an evening's entertaining reading. It is definitely not for people with unlimited resources who can wave a golden wand and produce an army of painters, decorators, drapers, and upholsterers to carry out their slightest whim. Nor is it for those who can decide over Labor Day to redo the living room and have it ready for guests by Thanksgiving Day.

It is, rather, for a broader group of homemakers, those of us who are gifted with patience and discrimination, who have had a vision, perhaps while walking through the design wings of a mu-

This is an expensive bedroom in an estate outside New York City called Exquisite Acres, whose contents were sold at Sotheby Parke Bernet in New York. The sofa brought $450; the low Chinese table used as a coffee table, $275; the standing lamp with the fringed shade, $150; and the elephant table holding a plant beside the sofa, $170.

seum or while leafing through a book on great homes, of the kind of home we would like to live in—if only we could afford it.

If you are one of those, the fact is, you *can* afford it.

If you are able to content yourself with something less than museum-quality furniture and great Impressionist paintings, if you have the patience to watch a room grow piece by piece over a relatively long period of time, with just the right chair and table in just the right place, then you can have the home you have always dreamed of.

It is the purpose of this book to tell you how.

Its thesis is a simple one: It is just as easy to buy good antiques and authentic works of art as it is to buy new furniture and bad reproductions of fine art. And it is more satisfying. Chair for chair, carpet for carpet, you can buy sound antiques for no more than you would pay for often poorly made modern pieces.

The living room at Exquisite Acres is furnished at a medium level, not down to our budget and yet not up to the maximum. This is only part of the room, but note the prices: The lions on the mantel, $850. The carpet, $2,500. The vitrine holding porcelain figures at right, $950. The pair of armchairs, $800. The tall bronze lamps behind the sofas, $2,300. The sofas, $2,100 for the pair, and the curule armchair at right, $400.

Let us look at it in another way.

If you go about it carefully and have a substantial income, you can decorate a Park Avenue salon for $287,340. Not counting pictures for the walls, of course. The paintings that would be needed to stand up to antiques of that quality would be extra—and very costly.

You can also furnish a smaller version of such a living room, on a scale that you and I would find more comfortable, for only $2,873.40—roughly 1 per cent of what furnishings for the Park Avenue salon would cost.

What you would have for just under $3,000 would be antiques of a different category, but pieces still worthy of the name. It may take you some time to find just the right pieces at prices you can afford, even if you know exactly what you want and where it will fit in your rooms. But if you are persistent enough to keep at the search, it may not take you any longer than it would take to deal with buying new furniture.

Once you are finished with the task and the pieces are in place, you will have furnishings of lasting beauty whose value will probably increase year after year instead of declining in value as new furniture does the moment it is delivered to your home.

The $3,000 budget figure is not an arbitrary one. It was chosen because it appears to be the minimum one would have to spend to furnish in a department store a modest living room—say 12 by 18—with what passes for good quality new furnishings. These would include a sofa and two upholstered chairs in an average quality fabric of the customer's choice, carpeting—probably wall to wall—a coffee table, end tables, lamps, and at least one side table and possibly a side chair or two, plus a minimum of decorative items—pictures, vases, etc.

For the same amount—under $3,000—you could have pieces that would approximate the ones you would buy new—a sofa, but it would probably have a wood frame rather than being overstuffed, two armchairs, a coffee table and side tables, and probably an area rug rather than wall to wall carpeting.

There would be enough money in such a budget to provide a picture or two for the walls. They would be authentic works of art, not reproductions—paintings by known artists or school paintings by students or followers of known artists, primitives by unknown artists who worked in obscurity, oils or watercolors, drawings or prints.

Whatever you would choose from the vast storehouse of legitimate fine art, it would be a serious work by an artist who has dealt to the best of his ability with the subject and his medium and therefore has given character to his work.

It would be possible, also, to add the finishing touches to a room furnished our way with a few objects of art—that broad and amorphous phrase that includes porcelains, silver, bronze, gold, some sculpture, watches, clocks, carved ivory, seashells, glass, barometers, and other old scientific instruments, netsukes—those fascinating miniature carvings by Japanese craftsmen in ivory, wood, or bone—buttons, bows, furbelows (showy bits of female finery, such as fans, headdresses, laces), treen (wooden household implements, generally handmade, or of a bygone day, a classification known in London auction catalogues as "Treen and other bygones") and a thousand and one other objects, all beloved of collectors some-

An autumn landscape by Théophile Émile Achille de Bock, a Dutch painter, $600 at auction.

where, all with value on a sliding scale, each distinguished by the hand of an artist or an artisan, a distinction which differentiates these things from the objects in the contemporary craze known as "collectibles."

The purpose of this book is twofold. Its aim, on the one hand, is to demonstrate the availability of real antiques and good works of

The point of this book is well made by these two chairs. At left is one of a pair of eighteenth-century George III mahogany side chairs with pierced vase-shaped splat, upholstered seat on square chamfered legs joined by an H-stretcher. They brought $750 for the pair at a Sotheby Parke Bernet auction, $375 each. At right is a contemporary copy, beautifully made, which sells for $695 without upholstery.

art at prices almost anyone in the middle-income range—low to high—can afford. On the other hand, it will encourage you, the reader, to embark on the vigorous exercise of your taste and judgment as you pursue the acquisition of such art and antiques to enhance your daily surroundings.

You must scale your expectations to what you can afford, knowing that if you can afford to furnish at all, you can furnish well—not with pictures of museum quality or signed furnishings that once adorned Versailles, but with reasonably good antiques and genuine examples of fine art.

How you furnish is a matter of individual taste, which is really a matter of whether you like pastels or primary colors, straight skirts or dirndls, linen or lace, solid-color ties or paisleys. Taste is highly personal.

Virgil Thomson, the composer and critic, once wrote, "All tastes are legitimate and it is not necessary to account for them." Your taste may not agree with that of your friends, your mother, or your brothers and sisters. It is yours alone. If your friends ap-

This serpentine-front Federal sideboard in well-figured mahogany, made around the end of the eighteenth century, might bring as much as $5,000 at auction, more in an antique dealer's shop. Similar pieces made in the late nineteenth century can often be bought for under $1,000.

prove of your taste, they may say you have a "flair" for clothes, or for decorating, or for letter-writing, or for improvising on the piano. If they don't approve, they may say you have no taste, which is just another way of saying your taste is different from theirs. What it all boils down to is that taste is often no more than a feeling or instinct for what is right for you.

If you announce that you are going to start buying antiques or paintings, you may be told you have "champagne taste and a beer pocketbook," which is not necessarily so. One of the advantages of buying antiques and honest pictures is that you can buy at your own pace and your own level. If your income is limited, you can squirrel money aside for that purpose and when you are ready, start looking for something that appeals to your "champagne taste." If you find something that costs more than you can afford at the moment, most of the people you are likely to be dealing with will set it aside for a deposit until you are able to pay for it.

More than anything else, what you need is patience—and time. The furnishings of a home should be what Ernest Hemingway called Paris in the 1920s—a movable feast. Most people finish fur-

nishing a room with a sigh of relief and a determination to live
with it a long, long time. Only a major milestone will shake them
from this course—a move to another home, perhaps, or the matur-
ing of children after the destruction of your original furnishings
has been completed, or a change in social life that makes worn and
unattractive furnishings no longer acceptable. Under such circumstances, the overstuffed pieces may be reupholstered, or a new
color scheme provided by slipcovers, new draperies, and that easy
answer for all floor problems—wall-to-wall carpeting. In general,
however, the intent in furnishing is to create something static, a
frame for the rest of one's days.

Inevitably, for whatever the reason, the time comes when the
need for change can no longer be denied, when a face-lifting just
won't cover up the scars because the club chairs have become
shapeless lumps, the down-cushion sofa looks like a mussed bed,
the front has pulled off the drawer in the library table for the eleventh time—in short, when there is no longer a foundation on which
to rebuild.

At this point your options as a homemaker are wide open.

1. You can go to a furniture or department store and replace
your furnishings piece by piece—a sofa and two matching armchairs (a "Suite" the salesman will call it), a copy of a "Biedermeier" chest, and an "occasional" table. You might decide that
your lamp tables are still sufficiently serviceable to warrant having
them stripped and refinished to match the trim on the "suite."

But unless you drastically freshen your thinking before you
start on this enterprise, the shape of things to come will be little
different from what went before. You may find that where you
had loose-back cushions before, the upholstery industry has now
learned to make a sofa that looks as though it had separate cushions, when in fact it is all one piece.

A new color scheme may offer some relief. The chances are that
your new upholstery material will be one of the nubby textured
fabrics whose nubs attract the oily black soot that is so much a part
of city life these days, dirt which responds to cleaning only with
an agent powerful enough to rot and destroy the fabric as well.

A couple of months and a couple of thousands of dollars later,
you will find yourself right back where you started—the same
room, the same kinds of pieces in the same places, the beginnings,
at least, of the same tired, shabby look, having done nothing more

than exchange old pieces for new ones which may well be of poorer materials and workmanship.

And the transition may not come all that swiftly. Unless you are shopping for the cheapest kind of mass-produced ready-made furniture which a Levitz or Ethan Allen or a local department store may have warehoused and available for shipment, you may have to wait three months for delivery, even longer in the case of the finest contemporary pieces. On special-order furniture covered in the material of your choice, salesmen promise delivery in "eight to ten weeks" but, when pressed, are reluctant to offer any guarantee of a specific date within the limits of that ten-week time frame.

2. You may feel you need expert guidance and decide to call in a decorator, tell her how much money you have to spend and plead for "something different."

In that case you run the risk of ending up with something known in New York City as Early Third Avenue Gothic—all heavy moldings and dark-stained hexagonal wood pieces of pine or gum that is grained and finished to resemble oak; brass nailheads that tarnish or come off; heavy draperies with gilt fringe; antiqued "parchment" lamp shades bound in leathern thongs, one panel decorated with a grandee's plumed hat, another with a coat of arms in reds and blues with crossed pistolettes to add a final rakish note of daring.

Everything would be color-coordinated, the blue draperies and wine-red carpeting picking up the colors in the coat of arms. Nothing would clash and in a month you might well find yourself fleeing your new and costly living room's discomfort and gloom to do your reading in bed or in the kitchen where at least you would have enough light.

If you decide to use the decorator services of the furniture or department store where you hope to buy your new things, you will find the staff helpful in the extreme and your choice limited to the line carried by the store.

But worst of all, it would be somebody else's taste, which may or may not also be yours.

3. The other option open to you is to take a solemn vow that you are going to do your home yourself, starting with the living room.

In your own taste.

Piece by piece.

*This early nineteenth-century New Hampshire sofa, upholstered
in embossed chintz, brought only $600 at a Cape Cod auction.*

Building it as you would lay a wall, stone by carefully chosen
stone.

So everything fits with a minimum of paste and mortar.

Leaning on no one for advice, accepting no help except from
those who will be sharing the rooms with you.

If that is your decision, then square your jaw, pull a chair into a
corner of the room, narrow your eyes and really *look* at what you
have to work with.

The sofa is comfortable and not too impossible. It was an extrav-
agance when you bought it, with a full reversible down cushion.
Suppose you had it rewebbed to lift the bottom springs off the
floor, professionally cleaned to revive the pale green velvet which
has now gone dull and gray, the down in the cushions taken out
and refreshed with perhaps another pound of feathers. Wouldn't it
really do for a while? As a start?

Of course it would. Besides, it makes sense. Starting out by
replacing the most important piece in the room would automatically freeze you into the existing arrangement—the sofa on the
long wall, lamp tables on either side, two chairs facing each other
across the coffee table.

So what else is new?

Perhaps if you make do with the sofa for another year, foregoing the cleaning and rewebbing if it doesn't seem worthwhile, you may find, when you have replaced some of the other pieces, that all you really want is a love seat for that wall, big enough for two. How often have you seen three people sitting on that sofa anyway, unless it is the only piece facing the TV?

So the sofa will do for a while, to be replaced only when the rest of the room has begun to crystallize, in fact as well as in your imagination, and you have a clear view of what should take its place.

But what about those lumpy club chairs? The framing in the arms seems to have worked loose so they are splayed out in an odd sort of way and look crippled, with the stuffing beginning to sag down below the arms. They could be called club-footed, they're so misshapen.

Out! Dump them! As fast as you can!

Suppose you replace one with a Queen Anne wing chair? With graceful pad feet? Upholstered in fine, pale green damask? A chair you can curl up in to read, suited also to a tall man?

Of the period? Not likely, unless you are exceptionally accident prone—happy accident, that is. A good Queen Anne chair from the eighteenth century would cripple the budget, but a nineteenth-century reproduction, in good condition, probably English rather than American, since the prices of all American furniture are on an upward spiral, would probably turn up at a price you can afford.

Yes, it would be a copy, but a very special copy. If it was English, it might well have been made by the grandson of a man who was making such wing chairs in the eighteenth century, maybe using his tools, working still in his old shop, probably following the same careful designs and impeccable workmanship, morticing the joints, pegging them with hard wood so the seat frame will be strong and the back firm and sturdy, using seasoned woods cut to the grain for added strength and a guarantee against warping, raking the legs where the style permits so they will hold a man, or a mammoth.

Maybe later, to occupy the space left by the other club chair, a French armchair—the marvel is how well French and English eighteenth-century furniture blend, a fact recognized by English furniture designers since the days of Adam and Chippendale who

This is an eighteenth-century American Chippendale mahogany armchair, made in New York, circa 1760–80. Similar chairs have been made ever since. Those made in the nineteenth century probably will be cheaper than similar ones made today.

made pieces in what was called the "French taste" for English sitting rooms.

A bergère, then, its name the same as the French word for shepherdess, a chair built to enfold the sitter as though between embracing arms. Covered in a sturdy French fabric that will last decades, sometimes even a century or more. Yes, they still make those fabrics in France, in the old classic patterns, and any good upholsterer in this country can find them for you.

But take note of how important original workmanship and materials are. In many an elegant French salon you will see chairs covered with the original fabric, threadbare, falling apart perhaps, but not likely to be replaced until the last threads have parted, because original materials are always treasured. So if you should be fortunate enough to find a chair with original fabric, worn and shabby though it may be, let the fact that it is old make you secure in its shabbiness so you can say to a critical friend:

"Oh, no. I wouldn't think of replacing the covering. It's eighteenth century!"

By now it should all begin to take shape in your mind's eye, from your chair in the corner where you are plotting and dreaming, looking at your room with a fresh vision, like a mariner on a voyage of discovery. Perhaps a small walnut coffee table just there, in front of the sofa and between the two armchairs, and if you can find one, a spindly-legged Sheraton mahogany sewing table with the sewing bag in faded old rose silk hanging from its underside like a disconsolate udder, to stand beside the wing chair, with a small Chinese vase (Yellow? To complement the pale green damask on the wing chair?) made into a lamp with a classic silk shade.

And this time you will resist the temptation to spoil the effect by putting a plastic cover on the lamp shade. You'll buy a feather duster and flick the dust off instead, recognizing that while it may stay clean, a silk lamp shade rots faster from the heat if it is covered than it will if the heat can pass through it.

And you will need some things for the mantel and for the tables —some old things, little chipped pottery pre-Columbian heads, the kind Central American and Mexican peasants turn up with their plows in a seemingly endless stream. With one good piece to hold it all together, a bit of old porcelain, or silver, something old and beautiful, something with a patina instead of a gloss.

Now, if this is *really* the way you would like to live, you should be ready to heave a sigh of longing. How can you afford an antique when a *reproduction* of a Queen Anne wing chair delivered by a factory last Tuesday costs $750, if it looks like anything? In a vile green Jacquard cut fabric mindful of old Pullman car upholstery?

The answer to that is meaningless, for it is the wrong question.

What you should be asking yourself is: "Can I afford the reproduction?"

If the answer is "Yes," then you can surely afford the antique.

2

MIXING STYLES WITH MASTERY

WHERE do you start?

If you have indeed taken the plunge, have decided to furnish or refurnish your home yourself, over a reasonable period of time and to your own taste, how do you begin? If you are young, furnishing your first home, you know you could ask your mother to help. She would be happy to do it all and you would have a dream home.

But whose dream? Yours or hers?

If it is going to be your dream home, you have to do it yourself. To your own taste. And the first question that comes up is: What style should you choose?

Italian provincial? That could be interesting, with one of those big sixteenth-century Italian chests—*cassones*, they are called—between the windows to use as a liquor cabinet. Fine if you can turn one up at a decent price. And maybe a painted Venetian corner cabinet in that distinctive, faded green. But what about chairs? And a sofa? The only Italian chairs I can picture are those terrible folding Savonarolas made for warriors to sit on with one leg outstretched because they are wearing a sword—great as conversation pieces, but not for comfort.

Georgian? That would be nice, rather stately, perhaps, but wouldn't it be better for the dining room?

Early American? Louis XV? Louis XVI?

Tudor? How do you decide?

Well, what about—Eclectic?

Webster says the word means: 1. "Selecting what appears to be best or true in various diverse doctrines or methods. . . . 2. composed of elements drawn from various sources. . . ."

How's that again? "Composed of elements drawn from various sources?"

Does that mean mixing styles and periods?

Doesn't that reflect lack of knowledge? Isn't that considered poor taste?

Not at all.

Some years ago the French magazine *Connaissance des Arts* published a set of photographs of a gracious French salon furnished in impeccable eighteenth-century style. The walls were of old walnut boiserie (paneling), the floors were covered with a fine Savonnerie carpet. There were outstanding examples of cabinetry and seat furniture by the eighteenth-century master craftsmen of chairs and cabinets (called *maître menuisiers-ébénistes*, and discussed fully in Chapter 9) on all sides, and a few well-chosen paintings of the period, with bronzes, porcelains, silver, and crystal completing the room's adornment.

But the focal point of the furnishings, the one element that all the rest seemed designed to frame, was a beautifully restored, highly polished, two-seater Bugatti roadster, circa 1927, one of the most precious of antique automobiles.

The French are notoriously rigid in matters of taste where decor

A Savonarola. The fabric or leather back and seat and the central pivot make it the original folding chair.

is concerned. The use of an antique twentieth-century automobile as part of the furnishings of an eighteenth-century French salon attests to the fact that even by their standards, good design cannot be faulted, that a mixture of periods and styles is not only acceptable but in many cases is highly desirable, provided only that what goes into such a mixture represents good design and good workmanship.

There are no longer any valid barriers of taste that rule out a mingling of styles and periods—Early American and Contemporary American, English and American, French and English, Venetian and Dutch, pre-Columbian and Gothic, or almost any combination of all the above and others, with Chinese, Egyptian, and Spanish thrown in for good measure. A brown glass hand-blown bottle from the John Barleycorn distilleries would go very well on a shelf with Peking glass and finely etched English crystal.

In fact, by the standards of current life-style, there is a kind of pretentiousness in striving for a room furnished in, say Louis XV, that would make such a room of questionable taste for the average American home, for reasons other than style.

Elegance, the kind of high style that is typified by a Louis XV room, with its hand-rubbed or paneled walls, bronze doré wall sconces, crystal chandelier, and Aubusson rug providing a background for highly decorative Louis XV pieces, can only be successful if your home is in a center of elegance—on Fifth Avenue or Park Avenue between Sixty-first and Seventy-second streets in New York, in a secluded estate area in Westchester, on Long Island, Connecticut, or in one of the equivalent areas of the big cities and rich suburbs across the country. A Louis XV dining room with finely inlaid wood and gilt bronze decoration is an anachronism in a nine-room contemporary colonial house on a quarter-acre plot in a suburban development. Such a room demands a chef in the kitchen, a butler, and a scullery maid, not once-a-week cleaning help.

So we have to ask ourselves what would be suitable to our life-style, to the level at which we live and entertain, that will bring a certain beauty and even elegance—relative to the drabness of some of our neighbors' houses—into our lives.

This can best be done by discarding the notion that we are going to furnish in the high style of any period. Instead, we would set our sights on the simplest furnishings of those periods and

ALBERT AZZARRELLO.

A corner of a Long Island living room. The glass table and modern Italian plexiglass and stainless-steel chairs come in from the terrace in winter to serve as a bridge set. The Queen Anne style wing chair, in the far corner, is an English early nineteenth-century piece. Above it hangs a Haitian primitive painting. The side table at left is Early American country; the glass bowl is Swedish Orrefors. What looks like a cream bottle filled with dried grasses on the circular coffee table is just that. The pair of chairs are French nineteenth-century reproductions.

styles, mix them judiciously, buy only what we like, what suits our tastes and—most of all—what will make us comfortable.

If you are going to furnish with the things you like and choose things which blend well regardless of period or style, you must liberate yourself from old prejudices and outmoded ideas, of which the prejudice against mixing periods is only one.

Another is that antique furniture is fragile and won't take the beating contemporary life demands of home furnishings.

There is no question but that a delicate little Sheraton side chair

is delicate, period. It would be a mistake to ask a two-hundred
pounder who likes to rock back against a wall to sit in such a chair.
He would not be comfortable, for one thing. For another, there is
a good chance that any chair so abused, antique or not, in time
would collapse. It is also quite true that if the legs of a French
chair are weakened by dry rot or wormholes, there is a certain
added risk of disaster. But wormholes are not indigenous to antique
furniture. How they got there is part of the story of changing
taste.

In any case, it should be remembered that an eighteenth-century
piece has already lasted for two hundred years or more, during
which it got hard usage in all kinds of homes and circumstances, a
record for survival which few modern pieces can be expected to
match.

Another misconception which is daily strengthened by news
stories about record prices paid for art and antiques is that only the
very rich can afford real antiques and works of art.

Nonsense.

The Cézannes and Renoirs that sell for $1 million or more are
the rare exception in the art world, even today. In the last hundred
years, since the break with the salon painters launched by the Impressionists, there have been fewer than three hundred artists
whose works, in at least one instance, in the decade of the 1960s,
brought as much as as $2,000 at auction.* Many of the works by
the same artists that were sold at auction in that period brought less
than $500.

There are hundreds of other recognized artists who worked in
the last hundred years, many of whom are represented in museum
collections, whose works today never reach $2,000 at auction, ei-
ther because their most important works seldom come on the
market, or because their style or period is not in vogue.

If we go back another hundred years, we encompass the rich period of the late eighteenth century and most of the nineteenth,
during which time thousands of painters were turning out meticulous scenes from the everyday life of the period, rich in color and
detail, that are now much in demand. Before that, we come to the
period of the old masters and the Renaissance, periods rich in works
by unknown artists, many of whom were followers of the great
masters. Often the attributions as to the authorship of such paint-

* Encyclopedia of Modern Art Auction Prices, 1960–70, by Christine Ber-
nard, ARCO Publishing Co., New York, 1972.

Italian furniture can be lovely, especially the Venetian painted pieces like this tall commode decorated in multicolor landscapes, wreaths, and floral swags on a cream ground. Often these pieces are found in a delicate faded green. They can be used to handsome effect in an otherwise modern room.

Georgian isn't always severe. These chairs are George III, painted in a style not unlike the Italian commode with which they would go very well.

ings are hazy, or even nonexistent. But from time to time a painting turns up that is identified by scholars as by a master, sometimes after it has passed from hand to hand as an unimportant work worth only a few hundred dollars.

There is the unfortunate belief, held by many, that only a "genuine oil painting" is worth owning. If the medium is the message where you are concerned, you can buy one of those ugly daubs sold in every city in the nation, which are unquestionably painted in oil and are in that respect "genuine." They are usually miserable, manufactured, muddy imitations of art in molded-plastic frames, and they are being foisted on an unschooled public by unscrupulous dealers all over the country.

If, instead, you can be content with what a work says to you, whether it is done in oil-based paint, whether it is a gouache, tempera, pastel, or drawing, or even a good print or a master photograph, you will find, for somewhere between $50 and $500, a work worthy of hanging on your walls, as will be explained at length in a later chapter.

To go back once again to that question of style, taste, and period, what you hang on your walls needs have no relation in those terms to the furnishings of the room. You can hang a Dutch primitive in a room furnished mainly in American antiques that also displays a leaf of sixteenth-century Turkish calligraphy framed in a brilliant mat.

Styles change. Tastes change. There is an old saying that, "Yesterday's trash is today's treasure." The converse is also true—today's treasure may well be regarded tomorrow as trash.

Only people remain unchanged. Status and the symbols of status were as important in nineteenth-century France as they are in the closing quarter of twentieth-century America.

A French housewife, living under the Empire in early nineteenth-century Paris, might well have looked about her drawing room with its outmoded furnishings from the decadent days of Louis XVI and have decided they must go—up to the attic or out to the barns (where the worms and dry rot came into the picture) to be replaced by the rich tropical woods and Sphinx-head bronzes of the Empire.

Just so, an American housewife living in Binghamton, New York, in the early decades of this century might have decided she could no longer live with her Victorian sofas and chairs and her whatnot cabinets and rejected them in favor of *art nouveau* or the

This is a steel day bed, made for use either in a bedroom or sitting room. Is it an antique or modern? It was made in the first quarter of the nineteenth century, one of many such pieces produced for Napoleon's generals for use in the field. Usually they can be taken apart easily and quickly. Michael Greer, the New York interior designer, had many such beds in his collection.

gleaming rectangles of Bauhaus modern.

Because this is so and because man is by nature a magpie, incapable of throwing anything away, we have a plenitude of riches from centuries past to choose from in furnishing our homes today. The Louis XVI furniture rejected by the nineteenth-century Parisian housewife and the Victoriana spurned by the Binghamton lady are part of the rich store available today to replace our domestic squalor.

It will take courage—even daring—to do more than dip into the vast potpourri of the past. If you are really ready to take the plunge, neck deep but not over your head, you must first, in a way, strip your spirit and your subconscious of the conditioning it has undergone most of your life from the superb marketing mechanism that dominates our home-decorating industry.

A painting of this kind can hang in any room, regardless of the style or mixture of styles. It is a nineteenth-century Dutch school scene, which sold at Sotheby Parke Bernet for $375.

The severe lines and style of this piece would suggest that it is modern. In fact, it is French, probably from the first half of the nineteenth century.

That mechanism is composed of all the elements that go into the structure of what we know as today's life-style—everything from convertible sofas and stainless-steel cutlery to Steuben glass and the artistry of our leading furniture designers, from our colored and patterned toiletry tissues to Naugahyde-covered sofas, from canvas sling chairs in the corners of our living rooms to the latest kits of do-it-yourself furniture from Denmark in prefinished teak, from Pop art and Op art of the New York school to the Golden Gate and the experimentation of the San Francisco school, from bits of burlap glued to canvas to magnetized, motorized mobile art.

All of the people involved in this enterprise, from the lumberman to the manufacturer's representative and the retail merchant, are guided by a single motivation—the search for a market. That is where your conditioning comes in. You are influenced mainly by the shelter magazines—those glossy, richly produced, colorful publications that tell you what is new in home furnishings and show you how someone is using it—and the Sunday newspaper supplements with home furnishings sections.

This is not intended as any criticism of the home furnishings press, which has its role and its function and in the main carries it out well. But publications in this category are supported by advertising and the economics of publishing are such that they must devote the bulk of their space to the merchandise that the mechanism must market. The antiques trade—strictly speaking—is not a part of that mechanism. Dealers in antiques buy advertising, but their budgets are limited and they buy space generally only in specialized magazines whose readers are interested in the old, not in the new.

This is why the home furnishings magazines, to which you would normally turn for ideas about how to redo your home, will devote editorial space to a feature on an unusually beautiful home furnished in priceless antiques, or to a layout of photographs of rooms furnished with superb new reproductions of early American designs. But it will not show you a room furnished with antiques that cost all together under $3,000 because there is no advertising constituency that markets such antiques and is able to buy space in the magazine to justify such an article. The result is that the pages of those magazines are largely filled with what is new in design and treatment, and we are all conditioned by what they display.

Another factor that makes it difficult for most of us to take the plunge into trying to furnish with antiques is the news of high prices paid for antiques and for paintings at auction. This has done as much to condition us to accept contemporary design and contemporary reproductions as any other factor. The news that a Chinese pot has just been sold at Sotheby's in London for $1 million does not encourage us to run right out to the nearest auction sale to look for a bargain in Chinese porcelain.

Yet the fact remains that the million-dollar Chinese pot, like the million-dollar Impressionist painting, is the rare exception. Most of the items that go under the hammer, even in the great auction houses of New York, London, and Paris, sell for under $300.

Sotheby Parke Bernet, in an advertisement in *The New Yorker*, once urged readers of the magazine to view an important group of paintings that were coming up for sale, including a fine Renoir. The text went on to say:

"Of course, we don't have a Renoir every Saturday. But we do have an auction every Saturday afternoon, and most other afternoons, as well. The average price fetched by 70 per cent of the lots is around $300. The remaining 30 per cent are expensive.

"So if you can't find your Renoir, maybe you'll settle for a Dufy at $20,000.

"Or a Duffy at $200."

Mark those lines well. They provide the outstanding incontrovertible facts which reinforce what I have been saying. You can furnish your home with style and flair, using reasonably good antiques and objects of art, at no more than it would cost to furnish with reasonably good contemporary pieces. And if you choose well, your furnishings should increase in value as the years go by.

CHAPTER

3

A ROCKEFELLER'S TASTE IN YOUR HOME

WHERE can such antiques be found?
At auctions.
In antique shops.
In thrift shops.
At rummage sales.
At garage sales.
At tag sales in houses.
And so on. With some reservations, all of these are at least occasional sources of useful and attractive articles of furnishing, but the main sources must always be dealers in art and antiques and auction sales, if only because there are more of them and they offer the widest possible choice.

Unexpected things turn up in thrift shops and at rummage sales. Often quite commonplace things are overpriced because they are in demand while rarities, unrecognized, go for a song. But this is always true when one is shopping in establishments that make no pretense of expertise.

Professionals have moved into the realm of garage sales and house sales. They put prices on things, often unrealistic prices, and will run sales for a family that is moving and wants to unload. In big cities where apartment sales are likely to be advertised in the classified columns of newspapers, they are frequently commercial operations set up to gull the unwary.

Often casual sales from people's homes, whether labeled garage, tag, or house sale, will be a source of odds and ends that are useful but do not really fall within the province of this book—glasses (nine red wines, eleven white wines. For some reason, probably reflecting a preference for red wine and therefore a higher breakage rate, there always seems to be fewer of those glasses), odd assortments of porcelains, lamps for the children's rooms.

But when you do come across something worthy of your developing eye as a connoisseur, the rules for buying are the same as in any other establishment. Look the object over with great care. Take time, if possible, to check in a reference book if you're not sure. Don't let yourself be stampeded into buying something because someone else is also looking at it. Better lose out on something you covet than end up with a piece which is not what it seems.

In the long run, you will find more of what you want in the shops, galleries, and auction houses. Since you may well be bidding against a knowledgeable dealer or collector at an auction, you may often find yourself out of your price class. The auction market, after all, is the place where experts and amateurs alike must go to find a point of reference to reinforce their judgment as to the dollar value of a particular piece, or period, or style. It makes its own determination of quality. There is often a divergence of opinion and therefore of price.

The sale of the possessions of Martha Baird Rockefeller at the Sotheby Parke Bernet galleries, on Madison Avenue in New York, provided a number of instances of such divergences.

Among the 728 items sold over four days, there was every conceivable kind of furniture and decorative object of French and English eighteenth- and nineteenth-century taste. The most important piece in the collection was a table made for the Marquise de Pompadour, a lady whose taste as a decorator continues to influence us today. This is how it was described in the sale catalogue:

711. SUPERB AND HIGHLY IMPORTANT LOUIS XV
MAHOGANY AND KINGWOOD MARQUETRY TABLE
                    Signed J. F. Oeben and R. V. L. (C.) JME,
                                        Mid-18th Century
The ormolu-rimmed, sliding top, *en arbalette*, decorated with a superb panel of floral marquetry depicting a central vase of naturalistic flowers above an architectural trophy resting on a concave-sided plinth centered by a floral trophy flanked on one side by an allegorical trophy representing Music and on the other by Agriculture; the scrolling, foliate, outer borders further decorated with birds and vines and the whole executed in various natural

and stained, finely etched woods on a mahogany ground. The sliding top opening in conjunction with the ·frieze and revealing a central, arched panel with a swivel, rectangular panel lined on one side with blue *moiré* silk and decorated on the other with pseudo-Japanese lacquer, the whole rising by means of a secret ratchet support, the border of the panel inlaid with floral marquetry interspaced by oval panels decorated with trellis marquetry and flanked on each side by a shaped, hinged compartment, both inlaid with bunches of naturalistic flowers within bound-ribbon borders, the interiors lined with panels of well-figured kingwood. The shaped frieze veneered *à quatres faces* with floral marquetry panels on mahogany grounds within kingwood borders, the front of the frieze containing a shallow drawer opening by means of a secret lever, the base of the frieze with an ormolu rim centered on each side by foliate, ormolu motifs and continuing down to cabriole legs. The corners fitted with finely chiseled, scrolling, foliate, ormolu mounts incorporating castle turrets above crossed bows and arrows and continuing down to cabriole legs, unusually pierced on three sides, fitted with molded ormolu *encadrements* and veneered in kingwood; the legs ending in scrolling, foliate, ormolu *sabots.*   *Height 27½ inches; width 32¼ inches*

Jean-François Oeben, M.E., 1761.
Roger Vandercruse, dit Lacroix, M.E., 1755.

Collection of the Marquise de Pompadour.
Collection of the Marquis of Tullibardine.
Collection of Mrs. Mary Gavin Baillie-Hamilton.
Collection of Lady Harvey, London.
From Lewis and Simmons, Paris.
Collection of Judge Elbert H. Gary, New York, American Art
    Association's sale, April 21, 1928, lot 271.
From Duveen Brothers, Paris and New York.

> The long established attribution to the original ownership of this table by the Marquise de Pompadour is justified by, first, the presence of the main charge of her coat of arms, i.e. a tower, repeated at the top of the ormolu mounts of each corner; second, the signature of Jean-François Oeben, who enjoyed the protection and patronage of Louis XV's favorite; third, the exceptional quality and the unusual mechanical features of the table indicating a major commission; fourth, the choice of the symbols of Architecture occupying the central position of the top marquetry panel possibly alluding to the office

of Directeur Géneral des Bâtiments du Roi which Madame de Pompadour secured for her brother, the Marquis de Marigny.

Jean-François Oeben was married to Francis-Marguerite Vandercruse, the sister of Roger Vandercruse, dit Lacroix, in 1749. The presence of the stamp of Roger Vandercruse possibly indicates that he either worked in collaboration with Oeben on the table or that he mended the table at a later time.

On the final day of the Rockefeller sale, the auction market ruled that $410,000 was the fair market value for Mme. de Pompadour's Louis XV table.

A few minutes before the Pompadour table was sold for $410,000, a Louis XVI beechwood *canapé* (a small sofa, in this case, of love-seat size, 3 feet 10 inches long) made in the last quarter of the eighteenth century, unsigned, went under the hammer. It was described as follows:

The oval upholstered back with a frame carved at the center of the top rail with a ribbon-tied spray of flowers and moulded with a repeating leaf design, the out-curved arms with padded armrests and acanthus carved scroll handles, and with similarly carved supports, the slightly bow-fronted seat rail carved with a ribbon-twist and the whole raised on round, tapering, fluted legs with paterae at the shoulders. Upholstered in stripe cream silk.

Doesn't it sound charming?

It sold for $450.

The $410,000, eighteenth-century Pompadour table was Lot No. 711 in the sale. The $450, eighteenth-century canapé was Lot No. 687. No more than a few minutes passed between the auctioneer's hammer blow that marked the sale of the canapé and the sale of the table.

The same buying audience that valued the Pompadour table at $410,000 and a moment later bid $270,000 for Lot No. 712, a Louis XV kingwood and marquetry writing table by Oeben, valued an unsigned eighteenth-century beechwood canapé in beautiful condition at only $450.

You would say the $450 canapé was a steal. But a lot of knowledgeable people thought the Pompadour table at $410,000 was a steal. Sotheby Parke Bernet's experts expected it would bring at least $500,000.

Mme. de Pompadour's $410,000 table.

The Pompadour table was an extraordinary piece, one fit for a museum—or for the home of a Rockefeller. But what will strike you as extraordinary about the sale was that Martha Baird Rockefeller, a lady of taste and discrimination to whom the cost of an object she coveted was never a matter for second thought, owned so many items—porcelain, silver, objects of art, furniture—that brought under $500 at auction.

What was true of the Rockefeller sale is true at almost any auction, except, perhaps, sales of relatively small collections, generally in one area, in which every piece has been chosen for its importance and its perfection. In the average sale, record prices may be set. But bargains also abound.

If you had attended the sale of Martha Baird Rockefeller's possessions, you could have furnished a large, luxurious living room out of the two catalogues for $2,873,400 or for $287,340.

You could also have furnished a living room for $2,873.40. Here are some of the items you might have bought on that kind of budget—under $3,000.

Let us assume that we were the buyers of that little beechwood love seat for $450. We might also have bought a pair of beechwood *fauteuils* (small armchairs) made in the late eighteenth century during the Directoire period, $700 for the pair.

A Louis XV provincial beechwood *guéridon* (a small lamp or vase table) 27 inches high, 18 inches in diameter, made in the mid-eighteenth century. It had a circular top with a raised rim and a similar shelf below. It stood on tapering cabriole legs of diamond section, which means that the legs were in fact diamond-shaped with a sharp edge of the diamond facing outward. It sold for $250, a real bargain. In fact, not a steal, but a giveaway.

An Italian carved giltwood mirror dating from the middle of the eighteenth century. The cresting was carved with an urn of fruit flanked by pierced interlaced swags of laurel leaves, the frame carved with a double bead and reed molding. It was 35 inches high, 22 inches wide. It sold for $200 and would look beautiful over the mantel, or over the canapé, or above the lamp table. Now let us add: $450 for the small sofa, $700 for the almost matching chairs, $200 for the mirror, and $250 for the lamp table—all eighteenth-century pieces, not copies or reproductions—total $1,600.

What else do we need? Lamp tables beside the love seat. A piece of cabinetry to stand against the wall, between the two windows. A coffee table. And things—decorative objects, pictures.

Subtracting $1,600 from our budget of $2,873.40, we have $1,273.40 left to spend. It will be close, but we can make it.

First, the coffee table.

Ah! Here is one.

A Louis XVI giltwood stool, made in the last quarter of the eighteenth century, lacking upholstery and now with a mottled gray, brown, and white marble top, a perfect coffee table. It stands on tapering fluted legs carved at the shoulders with paterae. (Those are the oval or circular medallions carved in the wood with a stylized leaf pattern radiating from the center.) It is just the right size, too—16½ inches high and 29 inches wide—to fit in front of the little love seat. Obviously Mrs. Rockefeller must have used it in some similar way, if not in that exact spot, $225.

Now the side tables. We could use a pair (not necessarily the

This Georgian bench—and similar French pieces—are often found with the upholstery replaced by a marble or other top so they can be used as coffee tables.

same) of Pembroke tables, or something similar. Here is a pair of George III style mahogany occasional tables, 26 inches high and 18 inches wide. They are a bargain at $170 even though they are reproductions, not late eighteenth or early nineteenth century, which was the George III period. But let us look further and see if we can end up with a room of authentic period antiques.

Here is a nest of four Regency mahogany tables, the highest of which is 28½ inches, also 18 inches wide. They date from the first quarter of the nineteenth century—$300. They are worth having because of the extra little tables that are so important when there are guests. And Regency is acceptable. Not that we couldn't find an eighteenth-century piece for that spot. There is a Pembroke mahogany table, George III, late eighteenth century, with flaps that can be raised and a writing slide and drawer, $400.

Here is another nest of four mahogany tables—late George III, about the same size and only $190. So let us use those instead. We could have one on each side of the love seat, the two tallest ones, perhaps, and stand the other two nested on the far side of one of

Corner chairs, like corner cupboards and cabinets, are much in demand. This George II piece, of the period, sold for $800.

the beechwood armchairs. Let us do that. They are only $20 more than the pair of George III style occasional tables and are of the period.

So far of our $1,273.40 balance, we have spent $225 for a coffee table and $190 for four nest tables. That leaves $858.40. We still have the problem of the space between the windows, and decorative objects.

There are a lot of alternatives for that small wall. We could use a George III mahogany piecrust table—$400—with something to stand on it and something on the wall above it. Or we could use a small George III tulipwood tilt-top table—$425. Or a George III mahogany occasional table "cross-banded in faded rosewood" from the third quarter of the eighteenth century, 29 inches high, 33 inches wide, just right for that space—$275.

Imagine! An eighteenth-century table from the home of a Rockefeller for $275.

And just think what a conversation piece a room furnished this way would be. With some guests you could simply say that you furnished the room at the Rockefeller sale and let them wonder what it must have cost. With others you could drop the smug snobbish pose and say you furnished the whole room at the sale for under $3,000.

But wait. We're not finished yet. There is still money left and things to buy. Here we have a choice. A carpet for the floor which would cost most of what is left, or lots of little pieces—Chinese lamps, a bit of silver, perhaps something from antiquity, porcelain for ashtrays—whatever..

Let us look at the carpets first and decide whether to have the wall to wall cleaned for now or replace it with an area rug, refinish the border of the flooring, and make do with the lamps and things that are now in the room. We have $583.40 left of the original $2,873.40 we budgeted arbitrarily for the living room.

Mrs. Rockefeller had two kinds of carpets—big, impressive orientals that brought prices ranging up to $20,000 for an antique Isfahan palace carpet, 26 feet 8 inches by 11 feet 9 inches, which would be too big for an ordinary living room, and smaller oriental and Chinese throws and mats that sold for as little as $125—for a Tabriz mat 2 feet 4 inches by 1 foot 10½ inches.

On the other hand, she had—probably from her country house—a number of needlework carpets. One of these is described as a Mazeltov carpet, woven circa 1925. Mazeltov is a needlework shop on Madison Avenue that has catered for decades to women interested in working needlepoint as chair covers and carpets. The Mazeltov, probably worked by Mrs. Rockefeller's hand, was 7 feet 4 inches by 4 feet 1 inch and brought $250. The materials probably cost more than that.

But there were others of more useful sizes—an English needlework tile-pattern carpet with a beige field and four rows of six octagonal tiles, each woven with flowers, 8 feet 2 inches by 5 feet 8 inches—$300. Another with an overall design of scrolling leaves and flowering branches on a beige field—11 feet by 8 feet, $900, and what seems the best choice—a beige floral needlework carpet 10 by 8 feet for $550, which would bring it just within our budget.

But if we should make do with the existing floor covering, we

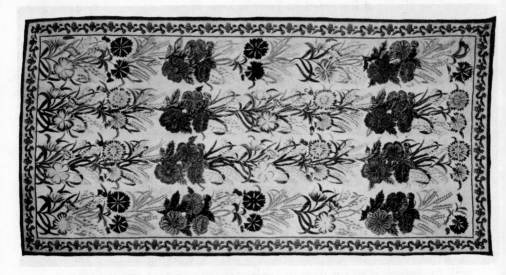

*A needlepoint carpet not unlike the one in the Rockefeller
sale. The minor pieces in such a sale are never photographed.
This one, from the collection of Mr. and Mrs. Ronald Tree,
is a Victorian piece, made in the late nineteenth century, and
it brought $8,000 at auction.*

could splurge on *"things."* An impressive pair of Chinese Export
porcelain beakers 29 inches high, mounted as lamps, dated circa
1790, for $525. Or a seventeenth-century Chinese five-color vase
wired as a lamp with its shade, 17 inches high, $225. If we bought
that to have one new lamp of impressive style and period, we
could afford a set of twelve Sèvres apple-green soup plates bearing
the mark of the Château de Tuileries and blue Sèvres crossed L's
with the datemark for 1844. Used as decorations on mahogany
plate racks these could be the beginning of an important collection
of Sèvres porcelain. Because they were mid-nineteenth, instead of
eighteenth century, they sold for only $325—that figures to $27
each, which is less per piece than you would pay for soup plates of
contemporary manufacture at Tiffany's. They could be used for
an important dinner party as well as for decoration.

The possibilities are fairly endless. For instance, a pair of American nineteenth-century cast-iron doorstops in the form of a horse
and jockey on grassy turf, 10 inches high, $80. A George III
square harewood tea caddy from the third quarter of the eighteenth century, its top cross-banded in rosewood with a central
yew-wood medallion, $110. A pair of George III mirror pictures
from the eighteenth century, 5 feet high and 44 inches wide, $375.

Another smaller pair, probably more useful, 21½ inches high by 16½ inches wide, $225. A pair of Regency cut-glass candlesticks, 22 inches high, $375. A pair of Sheffield plated oval waiters 7 inches long, just the size for the butler to serve you your evening cocktail, $140. Or a Sheffield plated salver, oval, 16 inches long, circa 1790, $120. All these are useful pieces for decorations in a living room or dining room. Or bits of quartz—four rose quartz trays, 4 and 4½ inches long, in the form of leaves, $150. Or three Chinese pale green jade dishes, the largest 6½ inches, $375. There were hundreds of objects to choose from, many under $300.

So let us consider it done. Whether you choose a needlework carpet or an assortment of objects from the list above.

And it all came out of one four-day sale. At the fashionable and formidable galleries of Sotheby Parke Bernet on Madison Avenue in New York, with an imposing doorman, in a green uniform lavishly decked with gold braid, to open your taxi door. Out of a collection put together by a *Rockefeller*. In four days. No fuss, no decorators, no looking at swatches. No dealing with snooty sales help who classify you by the worn spot on the sleeve of your mother's hand-me-down mink that you wear in wet weather for shopping.

In four days? No. Five. One more day for looking and measuring at the presale exhibition, for checking the estimates which now are printed with each catalogue, for adding up and readding the figures to get the most for your money. A worthwhile week of shopping, you could call it.

Think of how much more it might have cost in time as well as money (not to mention wear and tear on the nerves) if you had decided to do it along conventional paths, even with the help of a good decorator.

One month? Three months? Six months? If you have ever gone that road, you know that time is an accordion that can stretch out endlessly, what with exasperation over delays, over orders that are not delivered, with how many trips to the textile houses and the furniture stores and the conferences and the talks and the swatches. And the shoddy work that so often comes out of the workrooms, with the gimp or braid not quite covering the shiny blue-head tacks, the slipcovers that don't quite fit, the sofa that arrives with foam rubber instead of down and has to be returned because you abhor foam rubber.

CHAPTER
4

BUYING FOR USE, NOT FOR A COLLECTION

IN SHOPPING, for our purposes, you are shopping as a homemaker, not as a collector, and there is a vast difference between the two. The collector is motivated by one set of drives and operates by rules and concepts that are foreign to the homemaker who buys things to fit a room, not an intangible ideal.

The collector, if he is serious, must be a student of his field. If he is to succeed in building an important collection, he must develop expertise in the realm of his special interest. He may be a generalist, collecting, say, eighteenth-century English porcelain. Or he may be interested only in collecting figures, Worcester, Bristol, Bow, Derby or Chelsea, or in covered dishes in the form of animals or fowl, or the tureens shaped like cabbages or cauliflowers, or the much sought after boar's head tureens from Chelsea or Meissen.

He might also be interested in the output of one period from a single factory—Dr. Wall Worcester, or the Red Anchor period, for instance, in which case he will not be interested in earlier examples of that maker's work, nor will he look twice at later pieces. If this is the case, he has probably studied not only the marks on the porcelain of his preference, but everything that is known about the individuals who modeled the pieces and decorated them, as well as all the little details of design and shape.

His concern, when he goes to an auction, or browses through an antique shop in which there may be a piece he needs to fill out a part of his collection is, first and foremost, with authenticity, and second, with condition.

Thus, his first question would be: "Is the piece really what the dealer or auction catalogue says it is?"

If it is an auction item, in order to study its authenticity he goes to the exhibition that precedes the auction sale, generally for a day

This lovely room is the result of an endless process of trading up. The early nineteenth-century butler's tray in the foreground was added to the room on the day this photograph was taken. The mahogany corner cabinet is late eighteenth century, the sofa is modern and the red-striped settee is nineteenth century.

Every conceivable use has been made in this living room, furnished almost entirely from pieces bought at low cost at auction, of the decorative possibilities inherent in a variety of objects. The books in their colorful leather bindings at one end of the room provide one dominant element. The plants offer another. The pictures are nineteenth-century European landscapes, of a kind available even today for a few hundred dollars. The upholstered pieces are contemporary, but the cabinetry and armchairs all have a certain age, giving style and flair to this well-proportioned room.

The Chinese carpet in this high-ceilinged living room is the only item in the room that cost more than $500 and it was bought from a department store. Everything else, including the matching sofa, came from modest auctions or secondhand purchases. The Italian refectory table, barely visible against the tall windows, is particularly fine.

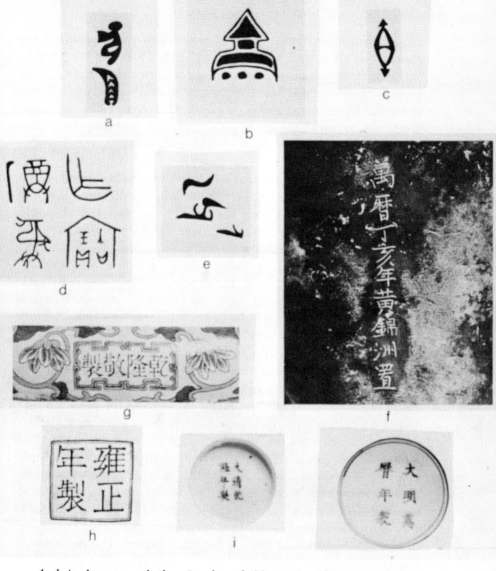

Archaic bronzes, whether for household or ritual use, are often marked with pictograms, stylized representations of Chinese characters, animals, figures, implements, whose meanings can only be guessed at. (a) through (e) are pictograms. Later works carry marks and seals which indicate the emperor under whose reign (and often for whom) the piece was made. (f) is the mark of the Emperor Wan Li. The characters in this case also give a date which corresponds to the year 1587. (g) is one type of four-character Ch'ien Lung mark which reads Respectfully Made for the Emperor Ch'ien Lung. (h) is the Yung Chêng seal mark within a double square impressed in blue enamel on a piece of Peking enamel. (i) is the more ordinary six-character mark of the reign of Emperor Ch'ien Lung, found on porcelains. (j) is the six-character Wan Li mark. All of these emperors belonged to the Ming Dynasty.

or more. He examines the piece at close range, using a magnifying glass if necessary, and satisfies himself that the marks are genuine and that it is indeed an authentic piece, properly catalogued as such. Strange as it may seem, eighteenth-century porcelain, Sèvres, and other Continental works, in particular, were widely imitated, down to the marks on the original pieces. A porcelain fabricator named Samson, in Paris, in the nineteenth century, was particularly active in this area.

The collector's next question would concern its condition. Is the decoration so worn that the piece is no longer truly typical of the Worcester kiln's work during the Dr. Wall period? Is it chipped? Has it been repaired? Are there surface cracks in the glaze? The answers to all these questions would influence his decision to bid and the price he would be willing to pay for the piece.

Rarity would be another factor. If the piece was extremely rare, the collector, once satisfied about its authenticity, would be less critical of flaws in the condition of the piece, perhaps being willing to buy it even if it has been repaired, in hope of being able at a later date to replace it with a more perfect example.

Then he would concern himself with the history of the piece. Is the seller identified? Is he a dealer or another collector? The reputation of the seller would be a factor influencing the price a buyer would be willing to pay. Where has the piece been in the years since it emerged from the kiln? Often a piece has been in the same family since it was made, and sometimes there is even a bill of sale or a record in the archives of the maker recording the transaction. Has the piece ever been mentioned or illustrated in a catalogue of an exhibition, or in a book on the subject? The provenance (history of previous ownership) thus is an important factor in helping to establish the value of a piece for the collector. The provenance can vary from a complete history since the piece was made, to a record only of the last previous owner and perhaps mention of the pattern or shape in a book on the subject.

The value placed on the piece by the auction house also will be of interest. A well-run auction establishment will provide a generally sound estimate of how much an item is likely to bring. Such an estimate, as well as the price a piece ultimately brings, can vary widely between a major New York auction house or a modest establishment in the Midwest, the difference arising from the level of the buying audience in a world art center and that of a smaller community. An auction house estimate is not an appraisal of an

This is a much-restored piece, basically of eighteenth-century origin, but so many parts have been replaced or extensively repaired that the piece would not be accepted by a connoisseur. But for our purposes, as a well-designed piece, it would be fine at the $525 top bid.

item's worth, but an estimate of what it will bring in a particular sale. In either case the presale estimate makes it possible for a collector to decide how high he would be willing to go to become the owner of the piece.

If the catalogue is vague in its description, the markings worn away or nonexistent, and there is no provenance, a collector may reserve decision until he has had an opportunity to research the piece on his own. He would look through his own reference library, which he has built up in the area of his collecting interest. It may be that he will find some reference in his own books that would indicate why the piece was unmarked or that might suggest a greater value than the auction house puts on the piece. This would raise the possibility, if its greater value is not recognized by dealers or other collectors, of acquiring it at a bargain price.

As a buyer who is looking for an object for your home, you would have a whole other set of criteria. Your primary concern would be with how a piece would look and fit into your home and how it would stand up, if it were a piece of furniture, under normal everyday usage. It may be that you are also a collector of stamps, wine labels, Battersea boxes, Staffordshire animals, carnival glass, barbed wire, scrimshaw, or any one of a thousand other categories of collecting interest. But even though you may have the instincts of a collector, those instincts would have to be suppressed with great firmness in favor of your primary objective, which is the furnishing of your home by acquiring an article that lies outside your collecting interest.

You cannot, for instance, allow yourself to be overly concerned with the question of authenticity, as you would be if you were adding to a collection. Should you find a small English desk that would admirably solve the problem presented by a short wall in

*These walnut Queen Anne chairs are fine contemporary repro-
ductions made in England, the side chair selling for around
$1,000. On facing page is an eighteenth-century original, dating
from the first quarter of the century. It sold at auction for
$1,100. A nineteenth-century reproduction would probably sell
for less than half that price.*

your living room, does it matter to you, really, whether it was
made in 1785 during the reign of George II, as its style would suggest, or a hundred years later if the price, look, and feel of the
piece is right?

The practical considerations of your need for a specific piece
must always be foremost in your mind. Will it look right in your
home? Is it a piece that will focus attention, around which you can
build a small arrangement, perhaps with two little side chairs and
something for the wall above it? Would a mirror look well there?
Does the spot need a little light that a small lamp just there would
provide? Can you see traces of grain in the scarred and dirt-dulled

This is the signature of the fine French eighteenth-century furniture makers, M. Carlin, impressed in the wood of a Louis XVI sycamore and hollywood marquetry serving piece, inset with Sèvres porcelain plaques. The piece sold for $38,000.

surfaces of the piece that would respond to careful cleaning and a fresh coat of polish?

These are the questions that should carry weight with you, not matters of authenticity and provenance that in another context—your collecting interest, if you have one—might be overriding.

But some of the factors that concern a collector would also concern you—for instance, price. You would be interested in knowing how much the piece was expected to bring if you found it at an auction sale exhibition, because that is the best way to determine whether it is within range of your budget. Given the presale estimate, you would then have to decide whether you would go that high. Whatever you decide, if it is a piece coming up at auction, you should set a limit and stick to it. There is always another day and another piece, perhaps one even better suited to your purposes and your budget.

You would also be interested in whether the piece was acceptable, within your terms, as an antique. You will have to make a decision as to what you will consider antique to mean. As you become more involved in looking and learning, you will probably become less and less concerned with the exact dating of a piece. After all, if a piece is not of the epoque to which the style belongs —eighteenth century for George I and George II, Louis XV and

Louis XVI—it should make small difference to you whether it was made in the first or the last half of the nineteenth century. (You just don't want to pay for a genuine piece of the period and find you have purchased a later reproduction.) Price and condition would be more important to you than the date. Given a choice between a pair of Louis XVI chairs dating from the first quarter of the nineteenth century that would cost perhaps $1,000, or a similar pair made in the last quarter of the century for $500, your budget would decide which you buy.

At many auctions you will find a wealth of modern reproductions of period furniture, French and English. It is often well styled and well made, many pieces dating from the post-World War I boom period. Such pieces are not hard to recognize. The wood has a freshness about it that is an immediate clue. Sometimes there is a studied highlighting of the finish to simulate the wear that comes over the decades in old pieces from the placement of hands on the arms of a chair which in an old, well-used piece will wear off some of the finish.

The inside of the drawers of cabinetwork in modern reproductions is generally varnished, a nicety absent from old pieces in which the dry wood is smooth to the touch on the inside of a drawer, but may be rough and splintery on the outer surfaces. There may even be a metal plate inside a drawer with the name of the manufacturer, and the finish is likely to be hard and rather glossy. If the wood seems old in the drawers, pull one all the way out and look at the inside framing to see if it is also old with signs of craftsmanship in the joining and with no modern screws or nails.

Hardware also gives immediate clues. A modern lock, or hinges, or drawer pulls would indicate a modern piece. But an old lock or other hardware would not necessarily mean an old piece. And it is difficult for the amateur to tell whether a piece of hardware that appears old is indeed old, since copies of old hardware are made with great exactness.

Purists will surely scoff at the notion that an untutored person looking at the wood in a piece of cabinetry can tell whether it is really an antique. But this book is not being written for the purists. It is written for the pragmatists, the people with a practical goal who want to buy art and antiques for use, rather than for display, at a cost no higher than new furniture, with at least a chance that their investment will retain its value and perhaps even increase in value over the years.

CHAPTER

5

UNDERSTANDING AUCTIONS

UNTIL RECENT YEARS, buying at auctions was looked upon by many Americans as a rather unsavory, even disreputable proceeding. There were strong overtones of disaster—lost fortunes, bankruptcy, sudden death, signs in dusty shop windows proclaiming, "Liquidation at Auction by Order of the Sheriff." It all seemed rather unpleasant, something one would rather not meddle in for fear of unhappy consequences, or simply because of a lingering reluctance to profit by the misfortune of others, as though an aura of the seller's misery might cling to his possessions.

It is quite true that when an individual goes through bankruptcy his assets may be seized, including his home, his furniture, cars, jewelry, and all other personal property, and sold to meet the demands of his creditors. But even this is not always the kind of disaster it would seem to be.

Not long ago the Internal Revenue Service ordered the sale of a collection of English sporting pictures assembled during the 1960s by a Wall Street figure named Jack R. Dick. Mr. Dick made a fortune during that boom decade selling investors seeking tax shelters shares in Black Angus cattle feeding programs. He got into trouble with the IRS and various creditors late in the decade, and his assets were seized for back taxes that totaled more than $1 million. Altogether, Mr. Dick told me, his debts amounted to around $3 million, approximately the sum he had spent during the decade of the sixties assembling his collection of sporting pictures.

The first portion of the collection, sold in London, netted just over $3 million which went to the IRS and other creditors. The remainder of the collection, disposed of over the next two years, grossed more than $6 million. Unfortunately Mr. Dick was not able to enjoy his profit. He died of a heart attack shortly after the first London sale.

The same market collapse that caught Mr. Dick ruined a small Wall Street investment house owned by a man whose wife was a collector of English silver. This was not a case of bankruptcy, but liquid cash was not sufficient to meet the firm's obligations to investors. So the silver collection was sold at auction, netting just under $1 million to be added to the pot.

The stock market is an auction—securities are sold through a system of bidding. The stock exchange serves as a middleman between buyers and sellers and takes a modest cut on each transaction, just as an auction house does. A substantial share of the trade in art and antiques is carried out in the auction houses, and only rarely as a result of a forced sale.

It is a big market. It deals with a vast volume of goods and grows by leaps and bounds. In 1967–68 this country's most important art auction house, Sotheby Parke Bernet, had total sales of $22 million. In 1975–76, its sales volume was $100 million. Sotheby Parke Bernet is the only U.S. auction house that regularly publishes its sales totals. But it is probably safe to say that the art auction business in the United States has an annual turnover of more than $200 million today.

Most of the goods sold at auction come from individual consignors. Probably the biggest impetus behind the art market is the dispersal of estates in response to the inevitability of death and taxes. Often the estate is that of an individual who, during his lifetime, built a collection of the things he loved and regarded his collection as a beautiful way to put money aside. Often a will stipulates that a collection be sold to cover inheritance taxes so that other assets can be left intact for their heirs.

Collectors are a restless breed and the more dedicated ones work hard at improving their collections. They are constantly selling off the bottom of their collections and buying more important pieces at the top, in the process known as "trading up." Sometimes, too, they find themselves running out of wall space or floor space while the collecting urge is still strong and then face the alternative of selling some things, paying storage fees, or, as in the case of more than one collector, founding a museum. Collectors who have mastered the art of buying at auction tend to sell at auction. Those who have had the wealth and the confidence to buy through a dealer tend to sell to, or through, the same dealer. And so it goes.

This is a spring auction on the lawn of a stately mansion facing Long Island Sound. William Doyle, the New York auctioneer, shown at center with hand raised, is a master at organizing such al fresco house sales. They are well staffed, with a tent for the bidders, catered lunches, and in this case, a splendid array of antiques.

Dealers are another important source of auction stocks. They sell at auction things that they have acquired which are outside their normal range of interest—French furniture obtained as part of an estate by a dealer in English furniture; the silver and porcelain acquired in a lot by a dealer interested only in cabinetry; the furniture obtained by a picture dealer whose reason for buying an estate was to acquire a single picture he coveted for his stock.

Dealers are also important buyers at auction. Until the growing affluence of the past two decades brought more and more private collectors into the auction rooms, the dealers constituted the mainstay of auction sales and, indeed, regarded the auctions almost as a private preserve. Even today, more than half of the volume of sales at Sotheby Parke Bernet is accounted for by dealers. The fact that dealers in art and antiques acquire a substantial portion of their stocks at auction gives the theme of this book an inescapable logic.

Why not buy where the dealers buy instead of paying the dealer's markup?

The dealer's price on an item he has acquired at auction is marked up seldom less than 50 per cent and often as much as 100 per cent or more. Because he is not dealing in an area of fixed values, the price he puts on an item is less likely to be influenced by what he paid for it than by what he thinks he can get for it on the retail market. A picture bought by a dealer for $300 which proves to be the work of a good nineteenth-century American or European artist is not likely to be sold for $600 if it is actually worth $6,000 in the market place.

Obviously a buyer is in a better position competing with the dealer at an auction, where he can buy a choice item for one bid higher than the dealer is willing to go, than he would be buying the same item from a dealer, even when all the dealer has done is to add his overhead and other expenses, as well as his normal profit margin, in setting the retail price.

All bets are off, however, when two private buyers start competing for one item at an auction. I have seen two women fighting over a colonial-style desk lamp, bidding the price up to $50 until the auctioneer, in some exasperation, remarked: "This is silly, ladies. You can buy the lamp new at Macy's for $35."

Auction houses do business in two ways. They sell for the account of other owners, which is known as selling on consignment. This is the general procedure at top-level houses, such as Sotheby Parke Bernet and at Christie's, now in New York. Many auction houses sell for their own account, in which case they buy large lots—the stock of a dealer who is going out of business, an estate whose lawyers do not want to wait for an auction sale to realize on the furnishings or other possessions, or, in some cases, the purchase of whole shipments from overseas.

When they sell on consignment, the auction houses reach an agreement in advance with the consignor as to the percentage of the total bid they will take as their fee. The percentage can vary enormously—from an average of 15 per cent at a house like Sotheby Parke Bernet where the quality of the merchandise and the resulting sales volume is likely to be high, to perhaps 35 per cent or even more where there is little of real value in the collection to be sold and the total for the sale is likely to be small. The consignor may also be required to pay for special advertising or promotion of a

An evening auction of contemporary art at Sotheby Parke Bernet in New York. The auctioneer is seated in the hooded podium at right, with recorders and clerks to his left.

sale, as well as for special catalogue treatment, such as color plates for full-color reproduction of paintings.*

There are also two kinds of auctions—unrestricted and limited. An unrestricted auction is one in which everything is to be sold, regardless of the price bid, without reservation of any kind. Such sales usually use the word "unrestricted" in the announcement and on the catalogue cover or heading so buyers can be assured that prices will be set by bids from the floor, rather than from the auctioneer's podium.

In any auction where the word unrestricted is not used in the description of the sale, it may be assumed that some of the items are being sold under a reserve price—a figure established at the request of the seller, usually by negotiation with the auctioneer, below which the item will not be sold. The purpose of the reserve is to protect the seller against disaster. He may say to the auc-

*Christie's has a policy of imposing a 10 per cent premium on buyers, limiting consignors' fees to 10 per cent and eliminating all supplementary fees to consignors except for packing and shipping.

tioneer: "I want a minimum of $500 for this pair of Louis XVI style chairs." In that case, the bidders are competing against the owner, rather than among themselves, until the bids pass the $500 mark. If the top bid is only $425, the auctioneer then may announce a bid of $450 and if he is forced to knock it down at that price the lot is really being "bought in" for the account of the consignor, because it did not reach his reserve. In that case, the consignor may be required to pay a modest percentage of the buy-in price to cover the auctioneer's costs in handling the item and cataloguing it.

No one profits from "buy-ins," least of all the bidding public, and it is ridiculous to charge, as some have done, that they are a form of fraud against the public. They are, in fact, an almost essential element in auction proceedings if an orderly market is to be maintained, no different, in fact, from the bid-and-ask price that is a convention of stock market dealings. It is perfectly true that through collusion with the auctioneer, a consignor can establish a false record to show an inflated value for a picture or an article of furniture, which he then can use to justify an unwarranted price at retail. But the possibility of fraud in an auction proceeding is certainly far less than in a stock market transaction, as the proceedings of the Securities and Exchange Commission show every day, since the bidding at an auction is far more visible.

The auctioneer selling for his own account may maintain his own system in which his reserve price is likely to be a universal one, rather than a reserve on any one item. He would have before him a sheet listing and describing each lot with a note beside him indicating his estimate of what each lot should bring in order to arrive at a satisfactory total for the sale, which will cover his expenses and bring him a profit. A good auctioneer would keep a running total as each lot is sold so he can adjust his expectations lot by lot rather than buying in lots that do not reach his estimate. If he has a piece that he regards as exceptional and the bidding does not reach his minimum expectations, he may buy it in and put it aside for a more propitious day and a more responsive audience.

Sometimes state or local ordinances may require at least one public consignor at a public auction, which is why we may see on a catalogue, "Property of John Doe, et al." The "et al." may consist of a number of consignors who wish to remain anonymous; then again it may merely signify that what is not John Doe's is the property of the house.

There are two approaches to finding at an auction the kind of furnishings and art we are talking about. Where the best goods listed in a sale are of very high quality, there will always be a few pieces in the middle range we are interested in—the good unsigned chairs that are probably nineteenth century, the watercolors, drawings, and prints by known artists whose oil paintings may be out of our reach, and so on.

The higher the quality of the best items in such a sale, the more it has been advertised and publicized as a big and important event, the less interest there will be in the unimportant pieces. The rich collectors and the important dealers who are buying for their stock or for collector clients, will be focused on the items worthy of such attention, and the lesser items may well go for a song.

Where the collection of a celebrity is being sold—someone prominent in films, or a dress designer, or a star of what once was called the jet set—other factors may take over. At the Helena Rubinstein sale, the Noël Coward sale, and the sale of the effects of Norman Norell, women battled to the death for unimportant trinkets, just to own something that belonged to such celebrities.

But at the sale of the estate of Martha Baird Rockefeller, as we have shown earlier, it was possible to furnish our typical living room with pieces that a collector would consider most modest, that had occupied a modest place in one of her homes, but which together would have a stunningly beautiful, and not at all modest effect in your home.

Auction houses are often under pressure to dispose of consignments with a minimum of delay, either because of the need to settle an estate or because the consignor for other reasons wants his money as soon as possible. But when there is no such pressure, the auctioneer will often hold pieces that are of greater importance than the average—one good piece of eighteenth-century furniture among reproductions, or one good picture amid a group of unimportant works—so he can catalogue them with like pieces in order to attract an audience better able to buy the more expensive merchandise. But even so, in almost any catalogue, there will be items that do not measure up to the best, put in to fill out a catalogue and increase the gross of a particular sale—a piece of English or other Continental furniture in a catalogue mainly of French furnishings, for instance. Often because a sale has been publicized as French or English, dealers and collectors interested in other areas will not attend the sale, opening the way for judicious bargain hunting.

Bidders at the more informal PB84 sales in New York are given numbered fans to hold up when they wish recognition of a bid.

There are three major auction centers in the United States—New York, of course, is the biggest and most important. Chicago and Los Angeles, because of the concentration of wealth those cities represent, are others. But in addition there is at least one auction house in every city of any size across the land.

There are a score of auction houses in and around New York, and it is a rare week during the season that does not see half a dozen sales advertised in the New York *Times*. Los Angeles has two of major interest—Newman's, an old and highly reputable establishment, and a branch of Sotheby Parke Bernet, which draws bidders from all up and down the West Coast. Chicago has four major auction establishments.

Important collections generally go to the big houses—Freeman's in Philadelphia; Trosby in Palm Beach, where impressive sales are held during the winter season; Hanzel and the Chicago Art Gallery in Chicago; Du Mouchelle in Detroit; Weschler in Washington, D.C.; Joseph Louis in Boston; Butterfield & Butterfield in San Francisco. A full list, city by city, is provided as an appendix. The competition is keenest at such houses. But for anyone who follows price trends at major sales on both sides of the Atlantic, it is always bargain day at most of them.

The pace and tenor of auctions outside the major centers is twenty years behind New York. True, the quality of merchandise sold seldom reaches the level of a major sale in New York. But the level of competition is also generally lower, even for the good pieces that turn up in most large estate auctions. This is as true in Los Angeles as it is in Cincinnati, in Chicago, or St. Louis. Once we leave the aura of the major art auction on the international level represented by Sotheby Parke Bernet in its Madison Avenue galleries, it becomes an entirely different game, one in which we can all take a hand.

CHAPTER

6

HOW TO READ AN AUCTION CATALOGUE

AT MOST of the auction houses around the country, your major
problem may be in coping with the lack of information supplied in
the catalogues. Often they are no more than mimeographed sheets
that start the sale off with "Lot 1–Box and Contents." They often
use a fast shorthand that can be confusing until you figure it out.
"SS Coffee Pot" has nothing to do with a ship's dining room. It
means the pot is sterling silver. Once you know that, it becomes
obvious that "SP Coffee Pot" is merely silver plated. As for furniture, "Antique French sofa" is about as far as they are likely to go.

There are perhaps a dozen regional auction houses around the
country that make an effort to identify what passes through their
hands and to catalogue it with some care. It is important to
remember that all you get in any auction catalogue is someone's
opinion that a picture, or a piece of furniture, is what it appears to
be–by the artist whose name appears on the canvas, and of the period that its style would seem to indicate. But even where the
marks on a piece of porcelain match those in a book, the evidence
is insufficient to warrant an opinion as to its period. Unless you can
recognize the differences in the materials used to make the various
kinds of porcelain, marks are inconclusive because so many pieces
were copied, down to the marks, in the nineteenth century.

Faïence–earthenware decorated with opaque-colored glazes–is
particularly difficult to authenticate, because faïence is made from
ordinary clay, and the traditional designs have been repeated ever
since the seventeenth century. There were potteries in northern
France, in the region of Lille, that made perfect copies of virtually
every popular style and shape, including the markings of the old
pieces.

Again, for our purposes, all we are concerned with is whether

Three pieces bought at a Cape Cod auction that would grace any American home. The Chippendale curly-maple chest on chest sold for $1,250. The smaller chest was $700. Both these pieces were made in 1935 by Wallace Nutting, the eminent authority on American furniture. The mirror sold for $400.

we are paying reproduction prices or the higher price of an authentic old piece. Many of the auction houses around the country have appraisers who do their cataloguing, who are expert enough to be able to discern the difference, and who will give you their opinion of a piece.

In the case of the major auction houses, however, and when we speak of this category we are speaking only of Sotheby Parke Bernet and Christie's, the cataloguers are traditionally *poets manqué* whose goal is to enslave your mind with an outpouring of lush, descriptive prose. The result is a language rich, mellifluous, pleasing to the eye and the ear, with a cadence and lilt that gives it a hypnotic quality well calculated to carry the reader off to the clouds.

So it behooves the buyer at auction to take a short course in how to read a catalogue—the words themselves, the words that are omitted, and the spaces between the lines, all of which have meaning to the discerning.

There is nothing careless about the language of an auction catalogue. In fact, each word is most carefully chosen, carefully calculated to induce carelessness in the unwary reader. Not, of course, to the point where misrepresentation could be charged, but just enough to encourage the unwary and eager buyer, to believe that a painting is what he would like to think it is, rather than what it actually is.

The experts are accustomed to this and automatically cleave through the verbiage to the heart of the matter:

"Is the article or picture 'right' or isn't it?"

"What do the gallery's own experts think of it?"

"Just how dependable (or marketable) are the experts' certificates that accompany it?"

And so on.

Whether in this country or abroad, usually all the information needed to decide, if not the authenticity and value of a piece, at least the gallery's evaluation and appraisal, is in the catalogue description. But it can be, and often is, most skillfully obscured.

See how you understand this example:

> Set of six George III mahogany side chairs, each cupid's bow cresting rail carved with foliage and flame ornament, the lozenge form, pierced splats carved with bow-knotted ribbon and scrolling foliage; the almost rectangular seats with shaped rails carved with C-scrolls and foliage and raised on bold cabriole legs carved with foliage and trellis design at the knees and ending in claw-and-ball feet. Third quarter eighteenth century.

The language was almost worth the price of $350 each. Reading such descriptions, it is no wonder one can become bemused and go off the deep end when the time to bid comes around. It also makes it rather difficult to cut through to the bone and absorb only the sense of the description, in this case of an acceptable set of George III chairs. What makes them acceptable is not the style, George III, but the line that reads: "Third quarter eighteenth century."

That represents Sotheby Parke Bernet's experts putting their reputation on the line as to the authenticity of the pieces as eighteenth-century antiques.

On reading such descriptions, look for the things that are left out. Omissions can be fully as important as all the other details of description put together, such as leaving out an approximation of the date a piece was made. A large amount of George III furniture was made after 1850 and while it may still be highly acceptable by our standards, it should not be bought at prices merited by pieces made in the last quarter of the eighteenth century.

"Style" means just that—a piece made in the style of a particular period, rather than in the period itself.

The major auction houses take great pride, and justifiably so, in the quality of their expertise. Houses like Sotheby Parke Bernet and Christie International in New York have staffs of experts who often would be qualified to serve as museum curators. Where most auction houses have small staffs—just what is needed to carry on the job of appraising, buying, and doing the often rudimentary cataloguing for the sales—the major houses have experts in every area, from books and manuscripts through old master paintings, diamonds and other gems, as well as American Indian artifacts. When a piece comes in on which the house experts are uncertain, the staff will not hesitate to seek the opinion of an expert from a museum, or a dealer particularly qualified in the area.

The auction catalogues of such a house, in spite of the sometimes florid descriptions, constitute a course in art history, design, and gemology. Often the catalogues, particularly those of Sotheby's and Christie's in London, are liberally footnoted, with precious detail of vast importance to a collector or student of a particular area. Take this one, for example, from a catalogue of Christie's:

47. MOSAN (?) CIRCA 1180. A GILT BRONZE FIGURE OF ST. JOHN THE EVANGELIST.
In an attitude of mourning, the head turned and supported by the right hand, the left arm holding the folds of a cloak and supporting a Gospel, the undergarment with a broad band of embroidery at the neck and sleeve of the right arm, the bare feet visible at the base.

3 11/16 high 9.5 cm.

This statuette was recently dug up by chance on a farm in Suffolk about twelve miles from Bury St. Edmonds. This extremely

Mosan statuette of St. John in gilt bronze, found by chance on a farm in England but with origins as to style in the Meuse Valley of Belgium, circa A.D. *1180.*

CHRISTIE, MANSON AND WOODS, LTD.

rare statuette, which would have formed part of a crucifixion group paired by a figure of the Virgin, is characteristic of the highly developed Mosan style which flourished during the late eleventh and twelfth centuries. Its naturalism of form and drapery combined with an understanding of the nude are a brilliant compression of the style of the strongly classicising figures on the brass font by Reiner of Huy, executed for the Church of Notre-Dame-de-Fonts (1107–18), which had a profound influence on twelfth-century Mosan metalwork. The naturalism of detail, however, particularly in the treatment of the face and hair, and of the embroidery round the garments, are not found in the works of Reiner (See the catalogue of Rhein and Mass, Cologne, 1972, pp. 238–41), and indicate a later, transitional date. A comparison may be made with the four figures of seated Evangelists on the crucifix base at St. Omer (Rhein und Mass, pp. 254–56) which dates from circa 1160–70.

In view of the provenance of this statuette, an English origin cannot be ruled out. The Mosan influence was very strong in England, and can be seen in such works as the candlestick given by Abbot Peter (1104–13) to the monastery of St. Peter at Gloucester (now in the Victoria and Albert Museum), the enamel plaque of the Last Judgment made at Winchester between 1150 and 1160 (also Victoria and Albert Museum), and the Balfour ciborium (see M. Chamot, *Medieval English Enamels*, 1930). There is, moreover, evidence that travel by English sculptors abroad had a direct influence on their work in this country (see J. Beckwith, *Early Medieval Art*, 1964, p. 198). Although no English sculptural equivalent to the present statuette is known, certain details, such as the awkward way in which the Gospel is held, would seem to suggest a misunderstanding by an English artist following contemporary Mosan models.

The research that went into those lines was wholly justified if not by the selling price—$88,000—then by its rare beauty. This is, perhaps, an exceptional example. But it can be matched almost any week by a short essay on the style of one of the painters of porcelain during the peak period of the Meissen kilns, or the evidence in support of a new interpretation of a painting of the Renaissance, or that used to explain the dating on a piece of sixteenth-century English silver.

Until the general public moved into the auction rooms in division strength a few years ago, catalogues were written in a code that was understandable only to the experts. There were all manner of typographic devices, some of which persist to this day, with which generally only the dealers and exceptionally well-schooled collectors were familiar. The London houses still use remnants of this special style with regard to furniture. A piece may be described in a Sotheby catalogue as:

> 50. A George III mahogany toilet mirror with a shield-shaped plate and three drawers in the bow-fronted base, on ogee bracket feet. 1 ft. 6½ in. wide.
>
> 51. A GEORGE III MAHOGANY TOILET MIRROR with a shield-shaped plate and shaped supports mounted with ivory roundrels, the serpentine base containing three drawers, raised on moulded bracket feet. 1 ft. 5 in. wide.

The difference in the descriptions lies not in the mention of the ivory roundels on the shaped supports, but in the capital letters used to describe the second item. They may mean that in the view of the cataloguer, Lot 50 could be a nineteenth-century copy, or has had repairs involving replacement of a strategic piece of wood, while Lot 51 is entirely original. Or it may mean that Lot 51 is indubitably by late eighteenth-century craftsmen. Or it may merely

A late George III drum-top library table, made in the late eighteenth century, which sold for $625.

mean that it is the more desirable of the two because it is of better workmanship and more gracious design.

If you were a London dealer or a knowledgeable collector of George III furniture, you would know by a glance at the piece what the cataloguer was trying to tell you and what, at the same time, he was trying to conceal from all those others who might wander in off the street.

This sort of typographical treatment is seldom used in the United States, but where it is still in vogue, as in London, it is used with regard to almost every kind of object. With paintings, there is now general agreement among the major auction houses on a formula to be used in giving the name of the painter, in order to indicate to prospective bidders what its experts think of the picture.

Because the system used at Sotheby Parke Bernet in its New York and Los Angeles salesrooms is the one most likely to be of use to readers of this book, we include herewith the Glossary used to describe terms employed in attributing the paintings:

GLOSSARY

The following are examples of the terminology used in this catalogue. PLEASE NOTE THAT ALL STATEMENTS IN THIS CATALOGUE AS TO AUTHORSHIP, PERIOD, CULTURE, SOURCE OR ORIGIN ARE QUALIFIED STATEMENTS AND ARE MADE SUBJECT TO THE PROVISIONS OF THE CONDITIONS OF SALE AND THE "TERMS OF GUARANTEE."

a "*GIOVANNI BELLINI"—followed, under the heading "AUTHORSHIP," by the words "ascribed to the named artist."
The work is ascribed to the named artist either by an outside expert or by our own staff and such ascription is accepted as reliable by the Galleries. While this is our highest category of authenticity in the present catalogue, and is assigned only upon exercise of our best judgment, no unqualified statement as to authorship is made or intended.

b ATTRIBUTED TO GIOVANNI BELLINI
In our best judgment, the work can be ascribed to the artist on the basis of style, but less certainty as to authorship is expressed than in the preceding category.

c CIRCLE OF GIOVANNI BELLINI
In our best judgment, a work by an unknown hand closely associated with the named artist.

d STUDIO OF GIOVANNI BELLINI
In our best judgment, a work by an unknown hand executed in the style of the artist under his direct supervision.

e SCHOOL OF . . . ; FOLLOWER OF GIOVANNI BELLINI
In our best judgment a work by a pupil or follower of the artist.

f MANNER OF GIOVANNI BELLINI
In our best judgment a work in the style of the artist, but not by him and probably of a later period.

g AFTER GIOVANNI BELLINI
In our best judgment a copy of a known work of the artist.

h SIGNED

A work which has a signature which in our best judgment is a recognized signature of the artist.

i DATED

A work which is so dated and in our best judgments was executed at that date.

The "conditions of sale" may vary widely in wording from one auction house to another, but they always have the same components. They are intended mainly to insulate the auctioneer against claims or law suits of any kind. The following is from a recent Sotheby Parke Bernet catalogue.

CONDITIONS OF SALE

This printed catalogue, as amended by any posted notices or oral announcements during the sale, constitutes Sotheby Parke Bernet Inc.'s (the "Galleries") and the "Consignor's" entire statement relative to the property listed herein. The following Conditions of Sale, any glossary contained herein and the accompanying Terms of Guarantee set forth herein are the complete terms and conditions on which all property listed herein shall be offered for sale, sold or purchased. The property will be offered and sold by the Galleries as agent for the Consignor.

1. The authenticity of the Authorship of property listed in the catalogue is guaranteed as specifically stated in the Terms of Guarantee. Except as so specifically provided in the "Terms of Guarantee" with respect to authenticity of Authorship, all property is sold "as is" and neither the Galleries nor the Consignor makes any warranties or representations of any kind or nature with respect to, nor shall they be held responsible or liable for, the correctness of the catalogue or other description of the physical condition, size, quality, rarity, importance, provenance, exhibitions, literature, and historical relevance of the property, and no statement in the catalogue or made at the sale or in the bill of sale or invoice or elsewhere shall be deemed such a warranty or representation or an assumption of liability with respect thereto. Prospective bidders should inspect the property before bidding to determine its condition and whether or not it has been repaired or restored. The Galleries and the Consignor make no representation or warranty expressed or implied as to whether the purchaser acquires any reproduction rights in the property.

2. The Galleries reserves the right to withdraw any property at any time before actual sale.

3. Unless otherwise announced by the auctioneer at the time of sale all bids are per lots as numbered in the printed catalogue.

4. The Galleries reserves the right to reject a bid from any bidder. The highest bidder acknowledged by the auctioneer shall be the purchaser. In the event of any dispute between bidders, the auctioneer shall have sole and final discretion either to determine the successful bidder or to re-offer and resell the article in dispute. If any dispute arises after the sale, the Galleries' sale record shall be conclusive in all respects.

5. If the auctioneer determines that any opening bid is not commensurate with the value of the article offered, he may reject the same and withdraw the article from sale, and if, having acknowledged an opening bid, he decides that any advance thereafter is not sufficient amount he may reject the advance.

6. On the fall of the auctioneer's hammer, the highest bidder shall be deemed to have purchased the offered lot in accordance with all of the conditions set forth herein and thereupon (a) assumes full risk and responsibility therefor, (b) will sign a confirmation of purchase thereof, and (c) will thereupon pay the full purchase price therefor or such part as the Galleries may require. All property shall be removed from the Galleries by the purchaser at his expense not later than three (3) days following its sale and, if not so removed, may be sent by the Galleries to a public warehouse for the account, risk and expense of the purchaser. If the foregoing Conditions or any other applicable conditions herein are not complied with, in addition to other remedies available to the Galleries and the Consignor by law, including without limitation the right to hold the purchaser liable for the bid price, the Galleries, at its option may either (a) cancel the sale, retaining as liquidated damages all payments made by the purchaser or (b) resell the property on three (3) days notice to the purchaser and for the account and risk of the purchaser, either publicly or privately, and in such event the purchaser shall be liable for the payment of deficiency plus all of the costs, including warehousing, the expense of both sales, and the Galleries' commission on both sales at its regular rates and all other charges due hereunder and incidental damages.

7. All lots marked with ■ immediately preceding the lot number are being offered subject to a reserve, which is the confidential minimum price below which such lot will not be sold. The Galleries may implement such reserve by bidding through its representatives on behalf of the Consignor. In certain instances, the Consignor may pay the Galleries less than the standard commission rate where a lot is "bought-in" to protect its reserve. Where the Consignor is indebted to or has a monetary guarantee from the Galleries, and in certain other instances, the Galleries or affiliated companies may have an interest in the offered lots and the proceeds therefrom other than their commissions, and may bid therefor to protect such interests by a representative or agent.

8. Unless exempted by law from the payment thereof, the purchaser will be required to pay the combined New York State and local sales tax. The rate of such combined tax is 8 per cent if within New York City and ranges from 4 per cent to 8 per cent if outside New York City but within New York State.

Deliveries outside of New York State may be subject to the compensating use tax of another state and, where a duty of Collection is imposed upon them by law, the Galleries will require payment of such taxes.

TERMS OF GUARANTEE

The Galleries guarantees the authenticity of Authorship of each lot contained in this catalogue on the terms and conditions set forth below:

1. DEFINITION OF AUTHORSHIP
"Authorship" means the identity of the creator, the period, culture, source of origin of the property, as the case may be, as set forth in the BOLD TYPE HEADING of such catalogue entry.

2. GUARANTEE COVERAGE
Subject to the exclusions of (i) attributions of paintings, drawings or sculpture executed prior to 1870, and (ii) periods or dates of execution of the property, as explained in Paragraph 5 below, if within five (5) years from the date of the sale of any lot, the original purchaser of record tenders to the Galleries a purchased lot in the same condition as when sold through the Galleries and it is established that the identification of Authorship (as defined above) of such lot as set forth in the BOLD TYPE HEADING of the catalogue description of such lot (as amended by any posted notices or oral announcements during the sale) is not substantially correct based on a fair reading of the catalogue including the terms of any Glossary contained herein, the sale of such lot will be rescinded and the original purchase price refunded.

3. NON-ASSIGNABILITY
It is specifically understood that the benefits of this Guarantee are not assignable and shall be applicable only to the original purchaser of the lot from the Galleries and not to the subsequent owners or others who have or may acquire an interest therein.

4. SOLE REMEDY
It is further specifically understood that the remedy set forth herein, namely the rescission of the sale and refund of the original purchase price paid for the lot, is exclusive and in lieu of any other remedy which might otherwise be available as a matter of law.

5. EXCLUSIONS
The Guarantee covers only the correctness of description of Authorship (as defined in 1 above) as identified in the BOLD TYPE HEADING of the catalogue item but does *not* extend to (i) the identity of the creator of painting, drawing and sculpture executed before 1870 unless these works are determined to be counterfeits, as this is a matter of current scholarly opinion which can change, (ii) the identification of the periods or dates of execution of the property which may be proven inaccurate by means of scientific processes not generally accepted for use until after publication of the catalogue, or (iii) titles or other identification of offered lots or descriptions of physical condition and size, quality, rarity, importance, provenance, exhibitions, and literature of historical relevance, which information normally appears in lower case type below the BOLD TYPE HEADING identifying the Authorship. Although our best judgment is used in attributing paintings, drawings and sculpture created prior to

1870 through the appropriate use of glossary terms, and due care is taken to insure the correctness of the supplemental material which appears below the BOLD TYPE HEADING of each entry in the catalogue, the Guarantee does not extend to any possible errors or omissions therein.

It is important to know that the price you pay at an auction is your bid price, plus any applicable sales or other taxes. If the state you live in imposes a compensating use tax on goods bought out of state, you may be required by the gallery to pay the tax. (*See footnote on page* 60.)

7

TIPS FOR BUYING AT AUCTION

THERE ARE no secrets about buying at auction. But there are a few simple, common-sense rules. You can ignore them, but only at your peril.

The first and most important rule is: Never bid on anything at an auction unless you have first examined it closely.

While this rule may seem to put a rather tedious and arbitrary limitation on auction buying, believe me, it does not. It is the only way to avoid mistakes.

First, let us assume you are looking for pieces for your living room. It is a room of fixed dimensions. It has walls of certain width, interrupted, inevitably, by doors, windows, and other architectural features which, for better or worse, are immovable. You've thought a great deal about what you want. And where you want to put it. And just how you want it to look. A chest, let's say, that will stand on the narrow wall between the two windows; a fairly tall blue porcelain vase, Chinese, you hope, with the Hawthorne pattern, to stand on it, holding long, graceful stems of forsythia in the spring and flowers from your cutting garden in the summer. Above this chest, tilted slightly out from the wall, a mirror to reflect the vase, the flowers, and a good part of the room.

The chest will be English, you think, with simple lines. And the mirror can be either Italian, with a dusky mirror frame, or American, with a flat mahogany fretwork frame, or even an ordinary English or French giltwood frame.

The space between the two windows, leaving an inch on either side between the edges of the windowsills, is thirty-four inches.

Question: How wide should the chest be?

Answer: Ideally, it should be no more than thirty-four inches and can be as slender as one of those graceful, slim-legged, marble-topped French pieces that measure about eighteen inches.

Question: How good is your eye? Can you tell from halfway back in an auction sales room whether the piece on the stand is thirty inches wide or thirty-eight inches wide?

Answer: Probably not.

Go to the presale exhibition. Take along a tape measure. If there is a piece in the sale that meets your style requirements, measure it. Height, width, depth. A good auction house will measure it for you and print the dimensions in its catalogue. Not so the little auctions which give you a mimeographed list that identifies the piece only as "96. Antique chest."

At some auction sales you will find that there is not enough floor space or aisle space to make everything accessible. If there is a piece that catches your eye and you can't get to it to measure it, ask one of the attendants to move it so you can reach it. While you have him handy, ask what the piece is likely to bring. Generally you can get a pretty close estimate of what you should expect to pay for anything being sold at auction.

If the estimate is not prohibitively high and the piece looks right for the use you have in mind, look it over carefully for signs of repairs. Make sure the hardware is all there—matching a missing drawer pull can be a painful chore. Since you are not buying as a collector interested only in the eighteenth century, look first for signs of good, solid workmanship. Pull out a drawer and see that it is properly morticed, not held together by nails. Modern copies of antiques generally have varnished drawers, particularly if they are well made. They were probably costly when they were bought new back in the 1920s, but they are not antiques. The gloss of newness will be on the finish if they have been well treated, and this will probably turn you off.

But if the drawers are plain, unfinished wood, if the wood seems dry and there are clear signs of wear on the drawer slides as well as signs of careful framing and handwork in the drawer cavity, then you may have an old piece. The finish on such a piece will have a silky sheen, the product of many years of handling and polishing. The grain in the wood will glow ever so faintly through its coating of dirt and wax.

Then step back and look at the piece. Proportion is what you are looking for now, proportion and style. Even without being expert enough to know George II from George III, your own sense of taste will tell you whether a piece forms a harmonious whole.

A living room in the Long Island home of the late Mrs. Harvey Gibson, just before the doors were opened to a horde of visitors who had come to examine the fine antiques before the house sale.

A drawer from an Early American piece showing the joining of the sides and the rough interior wood.

Scene during the exhibition at the Gibson house sale.

A bad marriage is as unappealing in a piece of furniture as it is in life—and almost as common. Say a dealer has a table whose top is disfigured in a way that puts it beyond restoration or repair. He has another which is missing a leg, but has an acceptable top. One is French Empire, the other English Regency. Put together, with the French walnut stained and refinished to match the color of the Regency mahogany, a piece emerges that might be credible to the undiscerning eye. But it remains a bad marriage and should be priced accordingly.

Look especially for differences in wood between one part of a piece and another. And for major repairs which, no matter how skillfully done, diminish the value of the piece.

Keep your eye and your mind on the action that centers on the auctioneer. It is easy to be distracted by the debate across the aisle between an auction clerk trying to collect a deposit and a woman who thinks she is being insulted at the request. Meanwhile, a piece that you covet may be coming up. (Sometimes pieces are called up out of numerical sequence because the porters have misread the lot number.) This writer recently bought a set of Queen Anne ashwood dining room chairs and was so distracted by the auction clerk's insistence on collecting a deposit immediately that the matching table, which followed, was bought by someone else. So it is not always easy. One way to avoid this is to go to the office before the sale, identify yourself, and give the house a check to serve as a deposit on any purchases you may make. If you do not buy, the check will always be returned.

If you do lose a piece you had set your heart on, you can often make a deal with the person who bought it, particularly if it is a dealer, by offering him a small profit on the transaction.

There really is no need to worry about having something

An exhibition at the William Doyle Galleries in New York City. The viewers below and on the next two pages are fulfilling the primary necessity in buying at auction, examining prospective purchases very carefully in advance.

knocked down to you because you happen to scratch your nose at a critical point in the bidding. Auctioneers respond to such silent bids only if they know in advance that they are to watch for such a signal, and even then, matters can go wrong. There is the famous case of Norton Simon, the California collector, who sent a letter to I. O. Chance, head of Christie's in London, arranging a complex set of signals by which he would bid on Rembrandt's portrait of his son Titus, because he wanted to announce the acquisition in his own time. The letter read:

"When Mr. Simon is sitting down he is bidding. If he bids openly, he is also bidding. When he stands up, he has stopped bidding. If he sits down again, he is not bidding unless he raises his finger. Having raised his finger, he is bidding until he stands up again." Not surprisingly, Mr. Chance got lost in this maze and knocked Titus down to another bidder. Thereupon Mr. Simon raised strenuous objections and Titus was put up again. This time, bidding openly, Mr. Simon won.

It is well to remember that once your successful bid has been recorded, the auction house expects you to pay for and remove your property with a minimum of delay. Some will give you as much as seventy-two hours; others want your property removed by the next day. Auctioneers tend to reject responsibility for any damage to a piece once it is sold, and since accidents can happen, it is well to claim your property and remove it as soon as practicable after a sale.

You can assume that an auctioneer will try to sell at the rate of approximately one hundred lots an hour. This would not be true of an important full-dress auction at Sotheby Parke Bernet, but it is an assumption you can safely make with regard to most auctions, so you do not have to waste half a day waiting for something you want to bid on to come up. In other words, if an auction is scheduled to start at 1 P.M. and you are interested in Lot 121, you are probably safe in getting to the sale around 2 P.M.

When there are two sales at the same time on the same day and you are interested in lots at both, you can avoid schizophrenia only by leaving a bid at one of the sales. Auctioneers will always execute a bid for you at the next level over the last competing bid. If you prefer to do your own bidding and cannot be on hand, some auction houses will arrange for a telephone call so you can bid over the phone.

Auction houses are protected by law against persons who bid and decide they made a mistake. The only recourse a bidder has is to pay for the object, then leave it to be resold at a later date, in which case he must pay the auction house's regular commission.

CHAPTER

8

TREASURES AMID TRASH

You will not find all the treasures you desire for your home at
the auctions. Many will come from rummaging antique shops and
art galleries, a particularly rewarding source in those remote areas
of the country where there are no auctions. But do not count on
being able to take advantage of an unsuspecting dealer who doesn't
know the value of his own stock. He is a thing of the past, at least
where conventional items are concerned. Even the lowliest dealer
in secondhand furniture has probably handled enough of it over
the years to recognize an exceptional piece when it comes into his
possession. And over the years he has probably culled out of li-
braries and boxes of books he has bought in job lots, a collection of
reference works on marks and stamps and even signatures identifying artists and artisans. Enough is published these days about the
rise in the art market so that he probably knows full well the
worth of his stock.

Still, the chances of finding bargains are good because of the in-
exorable workings of that old law of supply and demand, particularly if you live in an area where auction sales are few, or even
nonexistent within your convenient reach, or where there are few
antique shops and little tourist traffic to provide a stream of
browsers with money to spend.

In such circumstances the law of supply and demand takes over.
Where demand is small, prices are likely to be pegged at a level
that will move the merchandise, rather than on the scale of real
value that would pertain in a more sophisticated market. A dealer
in a small city who buys a piece for X dollars, may be quite willing
to sell it for X times two even though he has seen a photograph of
a piece in a magazine very much like the one he is selling, saying
that it sold in a New York auction for X times 100. Unless he is an

incurable optimist, he tends to discount the possibility that his piece is an exact duplicate of the one that sold for a hundred times what he paid. Or he may have the simple merchant's philosophy, which seeks only a reasonable profit over his purchase price, and rapid turnover. After all, there is no point in asking $5,000 for a piece when he knows he would have trouble finding a customer with as much as $500 to spend. Nor does he have the time or the opportunity, in many cases, to pass a piece along on a consignment basis to another dealer in a larger city, who may have a better-heeled class of clients. So he buys and sells at a price responsive to the laws of supply and demand that govern his own business and says, "If someone else can make more on the piece, more power to him."

There are, however, areas where individual dealers are less likely to be knowledgeable. Almost any dealer might discount the true value of a little broach in gold filigree with a chipped enamel sail-boat, a few seed pearls, and some bits of colored stone, and put a $100 price tag on a piece of valuable renaissance jewelry he bought in a lot of collar buttons and cuff links for $10, only because he has tested the metal and found it was gold.

Then there are also certain common-sense factors that have to do with local styles and tastes, as well as with the character of the trade of a particular shop, not to mention the kind of merchandise that habitually comes to hand in any dealer's ordinary day of buying and selling.

Let's look at it this way. Colonial American furniture abounds in what were the thirteen original states of Northeastern America. The East Coast seaports were also the places where English furniture arrived in quantity in the decades before and after independence, and where French furniture has arrived in a steady stream for two centuries.

Most of such furnishings stayed in the major centers of the East, although the pioneers carried their belongings westward with them —much as the latter-day itinerants of corporate life today are doing—and the nineteenth century saw the establishment of stately homes in all the growing cities of a burgeoning continent. For those reasons, almost anything is likely to turn up almost anywhere in the country in a used furniture mart or an auction house, as the stately homes disappear.

But the young executive who transports his household belongings to a new branch office in Southern California is likely to find

While Victorian furniture is going up in price, it still has not reached the level of Colonial pieces. This American nineteenth-century walnut bureau and the commode with a white Vermont marble top brought $275 each at auction.

that his English and French furnishings, just right in the rambling, Connecticut clapboard house he inherited from his parents, are strangely out of place in a California ranch-style split-level stucco open-living, indoor-outdoor structure with a free-form pool in the garden—the West Coast equivalent of his Down East home.

The chests are all too tall, the mahogany and walnut tables and cabinets inlaid with fine veneers are incongruous against the exotic decor designed for massive redwood and Spanish Colonial. His wife struggles bravely against the inevitable, shifting pieces around from wall to wall and room to room, then, shedding a tear, surrenders, calls in a dealer, sells the lot for less than the shipping cost from the East, and plunges enthusiastically into the task of refurnishing in a life-style befitting her new surroundings.

Modify that extreme picture just a little and it will accommodate a great many moves and a great many situations that are the life's blood of the secondhand furniture dealer's existence.

On the West Coast, the dealer's stock is likely to be dominated by the personal or household effects suited to the local life-style—at one extreme smoked mirrors in rococo gilt frames of Hollywood elegance, at the other, studio beds and canvas sling chairs. His chances of selling a carload of French and English furniture is limited by the same factors that brought the lot to him in the first place: its basic unsuitability. So he pushes it back in a corner and waits hopefully for the day when someone who is being moved back East by his company, and who has the wit to know that Spanish Colonial just won't go on New York's Upper East Side, comes in and he can make a decent trade.

Wherever you happen to be, in any of the fifty states, your local antique shops will be characterized to a greater or lesser degree by the local life-style and taste. Each dealer is likely to have an area in which he considers himself something of a specialist, even if it is in nothing more impressive than carnival glass. If his windows are full of the glass pieces that were given away during the depression to stimulate trade at the movie house, it is just possible that the dealer will undervalue an old piece of Bohemian glass or English crystal, classing it in roughly the same price range as a good piece of American cut glass, though it would bring several hundred dollars at an auction back East or at a Fifty-seventh Street dealer's shop in New York City.

So you have a rule of thumb. If it's bargains you want, look for things that are outside the shop's main interest, for things that may seem rather outlandish in terms of taste and the life-style of a particular region. But don't blame this book if the shop you wander into is owned by a true antiquary who knows, loves, and cherishes

RICHARD A. BOURNE, INC.

Rockers like these are to be found in little antique shops all over the country. From left, they sold for $135, $145, and $200.

everything, who can recite the Chinese dynasties and reigns backward and forward with dates, and knows by heart all the variations on Meissen's crossed swords porcelain marks. Such dealers exist, too, in surprising numbers and in some of the most out of the way communities. If you get a bargain from one of them, it is likely to be because of the sheer joy you have shown in looking over his wares and the disappointment in your face when you hear the price of something you feel you must have. Because above all, such lovers of man's handiwork are also likely to be lovers of mankind.

You may also encounter some churl—particularly if you demonstrate superior knowledge—who will be suspicious of you because you are not typical of his customers. He may refuse to sell you a piece you have fastened on, in the belief that if you want it, it must be worth a lot more than he is asking (which may well be the case). This writer recently wandered into a village repair shop which specialized in fixing vacuum cleaners and other small ap-

ALBERT AZZARRELLO.

One view of the interior of the Cracker Barrel, a Huntington, Long Island, dealer in secondhand furnishings. Knowledgeable antique dealers within a radius of fifty miles or more make weekly visits to walk through the Cracker Barrel because, as one put it, "You never know what you will find."

pliances, but also repaired and dealt in old clocks. Among the clocks in the shop, mainly late nineteenth- and early twentieth-century wall pieces whose original wooden or brass works had long since been replaced by electric motors, there was a small bracket clock with a case of mahogany, brass, and tortoise shell whose mechanism, almost as small as a watch movement, had a finely tooled back of gold and the signature of a Munich watchmaker of the eighteenth century. The shop owner took the clock from the display case and allowed me to examine it, but when he saw me reach for the price tag, which said $400, he reached for the piece saying, "It's not for sale. I haven't finished checking on it yet." A week later I sent a friend into the shop. The piece was back in the case,

Another view of the Cracker Barrel, Huntington, Long Island, show-ing the display cases filled with bric-a-brac which changes con-stantly. Mostly it is of little value, but occasionally good pieces are to be found in such a display.

the price tag unchanged, and this time the dealer sold it without a murmur.

If the dealer had had any accurate means of checking the cur-rent market value of the clock, he would probably have been told it was worth at least $2,000—a price far in excess of anything he could hope to get for it from the customers that were likely to pass through his shop.

Schooling oneself to really look at things is important if you are going to browse through antique shops. It is all too easy to walk through a shop letting one's glance pass from object to object without really *seeing* anything. It takes a conscious effort of con-centration to see and register on the brain the things one is looking

One end of the unheated, barnlike back room of the Cracker Barrel, Huntington, Long Island, where the poorest merchandise is stored. Note the carpet. It is a needlework piece needing repairs, roughly 8 by 10 feet, which could be bought for $50. The two prints high on the back wall are reproductions of paintings by Moses Soyer, commercial lithographs of no great value but certainly worth the $15 price tag on each.

at—a little like that first hard look you have taken at your own living room to really see it as it is and as it could be.

Part of learning to see things is learning to feel them. When you take an object in your hands, your eyes tend to come really into focus on it and the two actions do fortify one another. You can see a piece of porcelain without really being able to tell whether it is bone china, hard paste, or soft paste. But once you have held a piece of each in your hands, preferably one after the other, the differences in those terms begin to take on meaning. Hard paste has a smooth, almost glassy feeling, more so than either of the others, presenting a hard, vitreous surface. Bone china, made in part with bone ash, is similar in feeling, but likely to be heavier.

Soft paste, on the other hand, is not likely to be as white as the others and will be rather soft in texture, due to the fact that it is fired at lower temperatures than either of the others. Soft paste is characteristic of early eighteenth-century European porcelain before the technique of making mixtures of clays capable of withstanding high firing temperatures was perfected.

To go back to the question of shopping, browsing comes naturally to most people; looking and really seeing often has to be learned. One way to do this is to stop inside the door of an antique shop and look around at the groupings of like objects that will often be visible from the doorway where they have been put to catch the eye. On one side the cases with silver and smaller porce-

This embroidery on silk of the arms of the Common-wealth of Pennsylvania might be presumed to be American handiwork. Actually, embroideries of seals of the states and the Federal Government were made in China for the American market in the nineteenth century.

This olive-yellow, quart-size hexagonal bottle is inscribed on four sides "Wheeler's Berlin Bitters Baltimore." It is a highly decorative piece.

lain or metal pieces, along with delicate glassware. On the other side, perhaps open to the window, tables covered with pieces laid out to draw the eye of the window shopper. Beyond them, the cavernous depths of the store with furniture piled ceiling high and chandeliers hanging aloft like hams and cheeses in a Neapolitan groceria.

It requires effort to keep the vision from bouncing off such a bewildering display. Take your time. Pick things up and examine them. Ask questions if you're not sure what things are or where they were made, or when. Ask even when you are sure, to see if the dealer knows, but resist the impulse to tell him if you do know, particularly if you might want to buy the item.

Recently a dealer in a small village shop handed this writer a piece of carved white stone about three inches long and asked what it was. It was a Chinese jade buckle, used to fasten the traditional sash or belt, and was one of several he had picked up in buying a lot of more easily recognized objects from an owner who was as ignorant of their use and origin as the dealer was. These buckles have a value of around $100 or more, depending upon the quality of the jade, the quality of the carving, and the age. The pieces he

Carved and painted model of the whaling ship Minerva *in fine detail, made by an American nineteenth-century craftsman.*

bought, thrown in with some other objects for a few dollars, had a value well over $1,000. I might have said I had seen them used as knife rests on a dinner table (which I have) and probably could have bought the seven buckles for $50.

You must always look beyond the pieces that have been set out to catch the eye. Look in the corners of the shop and under things, for grimy, clumsy-looking little bronze pots that just might be Han Dynasty Chinese. But keep in mind that dealers can also be shrewd enough to put a questionable antique back in a corner and let it gather a thick coat of dust, waiting for it to be "discovered" by an unwary shopper who may think he has found a sleeper.

Having said all that, let it now be added that the antique shops are still not the best primary source of the kind of furnishings you may need to redo your rooms at low cost. The big source of the kind of furnishings we have been talking about remains the auction sale, if only because you just might find everything your heart desires at one sale, or enough so you can then fill in from the antique shops.

One question remains. Where did it all come from?

The early American sideboard was black with the grime of nearly 200 years when it was bought. Neither the grain of the fine mahogany nor the detail of inlay was visible. A splash board had been added at some point in the nineteenth century, probably at the same time that the original oval brasses were replaced with nineteenth-century acorn brasses. Tacked inside was a label dating the piece as 1790. The wall sconces of delicately wrought iron, recently repainted, are probably French. The watercolor is Haitian, by Armin Joseph, and cost $15 in an antique shop on Long Island just days before the photograph was taken.

The grouping of miniatures above this English desk is highly effective. And the miniatures were collected over a long period, often for a few dollars, the arrangement changing as miniatures were added. Miniatures are to be found in almost any little antique shop and since the names of the great miniaturists are not generally familiar, prices tend to be low. Often the quality of the frame, whether the painting is on ivory or metal, will be a factor.

*The Sheffield chandelier in this small but handsome dining
room was dewired, polished and fitted with candles. Of the
other pieces in the room only the armchair at right and the
tall etageres that flank the windows are antiques. The table
and chairs are relatively recent reproductions, well styled,
but not old.*

"Things" in a living-room cabinet. A set of porcelain plates are accompanied by bits of jade and other carved stone, Peking glass, modest clay pieces from antiquity.

CHAPTER

9

THE EIGHTEENTH-CENTURY CRAFTSMEN

In eighteenth-century Paris the workshops of many of the cabinet-makers (*ébénistes*) and chairmakers (*menuisiers*) who worked for the kings of France and the members of their courts were situated along the right bank of the Seine in the area known as *le Marais*—the Swamp—so called because of the periodic floods and seepage from the river that left the rough paving blocks and the walls of buildings coated with silt and gleaming with dampness through much of the year.

They came from the ranks of those who were admitted to the Corporation des Menuisiers-Ebenistes, the Parisian guild of furniture master craftsmen. The craft unions of the AFL-CIO, such as the engravers, electricians, carpenters, paperhangers, and others that limit their membership in order to maintain control over the labor market, could have taken lessons from the French guild of furniture makers.

Admission as a master was the highest achievement a practitioner of the craft could ever hope to reach. This professional pinnacle became possible only after at least six years of service as an apprentice without pay and an indeterminate period in a kind of craft-guild purgatory that could extend for a lifetime. Only by submitting a piece of furniture of his own design and construction, known as his masterwork or *chef d'oeuvre* (which is where that expression comes from) to a special committee of the guild which had to approve his design and craftsmanship, could he be admitted as a *maître* or master craftsman, and then only if there was an opening in the guild's tightly controlled ranks.

There was a strict system of preference for membership based on the hierarchy of the guild, with sons of the *jurands*—members of the admissions jury—given first preference and sons of the

*These little French tables—guér-
idon, they are called—are highly
useful and decorative and when
they are of the epoch of their design, can be very costly. This
piece, in the Directoire style, was
signed by its maker, C. Gaudet, in
the late eighteenth century. It has
a Carrara marble top with a
pierced ormolu gallery, which can
be raised and lowered on a ratchet.
It sold for $1,300 and its value
since that sale has probably increased by 50 per cent.*

masters second. Each applicant had to pay a fee for his training,
with the sons of jury members paying the smallest amounts and
foreign apprentices the highest.

The guild was formed in 1720 with 985 members. It still had
only 985 members when it was disbanded in 1790, in an act of revolutionary zeal which sought to erase every vestige of privilege
conferred by the Bourbon kings. The names of all the members
were carefully preserved with the dates of their admissions as
masters and may still be examined in the archives of the Biblio-
thèque Nationale in Paris.

Admission as a master carried with it the right to stamp the
maker's name on furniture and his status as master, with the initials

J.M.E. (for *jurand maître ébéniste*) or just M.E. beside the name.

Thus there were for sixty-seven years roughly one thousand recognized masters of the craft at all times during that period, representing sixty-seven thousand man-years, at work mainly in Paris, but also in the provincial capitals around France. Each of these men had in his shop apprentices and assistants known as *compagnons*. Although often they were gifted craftsmen, these men may have failed to become masters, either because they could never afford the high fees or because they were too far down in the preferential lists ever to have a chance at a vacancy.

Many of these craftsmen set up their own shops and made furniture in the styles of the masters from whom they had learned their craft, for the lesser members of the court and for the growing number of entrepreneurs (wheelers and dealers, we might call them) who carried on the business of the kings and the administration of the country's increasingly complex affairs.

In this way the craft proliferated and grew. Over the years, as sons were born and trained under their fathers, the output of unmarked and unidentified pieces, often of fine workmanship and excellent style, increased. Though the guild was abolished in 1790, the workshops continued turning out furniture in the Louis XV and Louis XVI style well into the nineteenth century, until the new fashion called Empire took over under Napoleon.

The prices the work of the masters brought from the middle of the eighteenth century through the revolution are meaningless unless some adjustment is made between the purchasing value of money at that time and money today.

The marvelously ornate desk made for King Louis XVI by David Roentgen, for which the king paid 100,000 *livres*, was the costliest piece of furniture made for Versailles. To gain some understanding of how much 100,000 livres was in terms of today's dollars, it is necessary to do some fancy figuring.

We in Colonial America were still under British rule at the time, but when the dollar came into existence as a stable currency it had a value to the British currency of four shillings. The English shilling was equivalent to the French livre. Thus, in terms of our money in the middle of the eighteenth century, the desk cost $25,000. But economists have arrived at an estimate that currency of the eighteenth century must be multiplied by twelve in order to arrive at some sound equivalency with the purchasing power of today. So we must multiply $25,000 by twelve to arrive at an ap-

This George II corner cabinet is a classic example of eighteenth-century English painted furniture. It sold for $1,000.

An important George III mahogany breakfront bookcase-cabinet is severely simple in design except for the glazed doors with "Gothik" molding on the glass. Pieces such as this often have stood in English homes on the same spot where they were placed when new.

proximation of true value in today's terms, which is $300,000.

At the other extreme, also from the Versailles inventory, is a commode in marquetry, unsigned and the maker unknown, made at approximately the same time as the Roentgen Bureau du Roi Louis XVI. It cost 210 livres, the equivalent today, by the same method of calculation, of $630.

After the execution of Louis XVI and Marie Antoinette, the Revolutionary Council ordered the sale of all the furniture and other possessions of the royal family at Versailles and the other palaces and châteaux. The sale began in 1782 and went on for a year,

*One of a pair of George II
mahogany side chairs with
an intricately carved splat,
which sold for $700. Con-
temporary copies of such
chairs cost more.*

disposing of some seventeen thousand items.* In that sale an earlier
roll-top desk, made for Louis XV, similar but somewhat more ornate than the one made for Louis XVI, the work of Jean-François
Oeben and Jean-Henri Riesener, was sold for 100,000 livres together with two corner cabinets made by Riesener. The desk alone
had cost Louis XV 75,000 livres, or $18,750 in currency of the
time. The three pieces today would bring at least $1 million at auc-
tion.

Looking at the $410,000 paid in the Rockefeller sale for the
Pompadour table, and the $300,000 value that would be today's
equivalent cost for the Louis XVI roll-top desk, it becomes apparent that the market value today of the Pompadour is really a modest increase over what the table must have cost.

So total was the Revolutionary Council's rejection of the Bourbon kings that taxes were remitted on goods purchased in the
Versailles sale, provided they were bought by foreigners and re-

*La Vente du Mobilier de Versailles pendant le Terreur, by Baron Charles
Davillier, Gazette des Beaux Arts, Paris, 1876.

moved immediately from the country. It was during and after the great Versailles sale that some of the important English collections of French eighteenth-century furniture were formed.

By the early years of the nineteenth century, the rejection of the taste of Mme. Pompadour and the other ladies of the Bourbon court was so complete that the fashionable ladies of Napoleon's day moved their Louis XV and Louis XVI furniture out of the salons to the maids' rooms in the attics, or worse, into the barns behind their châteaux. There they lay undisturbed for decades until interest revived in the last quarter of the nineteenth century when the Hamilton Palace sale at Christie's in London in 1882

This serpentine-fronted mahogany dressing chest dates from the George II period, the second quarter of the eighteenth century. It sold for $900.

brought prices for French eighteenth-century furniture to a new peak. It was, as we have said, during this unfortunate interlude that the worms got in their work and extensive restoration was done on some of the furniture that survived the neglect of those years.

All this is for the record and of only passing interest to those of us concerned with furnishings we can buy at reasonable prices to use in our modest homes. What is of more interest to us is that the master craftsmen of the eighteenth century, their followers and their descendants, continued making furniture in the prerevolutionary fashion well into the nineteenth century, and the production of copies of eighteenth-century furniture continues right up to today.

Some of the old-style workshops still exist, turning out an endless stream of chairs and sofas, desks and chests, love seats and commodes, in all sizes, shapes, and styles of the eighteenth century, exquisitely designed and fashioned from old patterns, in fine inlays of woods from Asia, Africa, South America, and the Islands, and walnut from the forests that once covered much of France. Some of the workshops are to be found hidden away in courtyards in the maze of streets off the Rue St. Antoine, between the Hôtel de Ville and the Place des Vosges, as well as across the Seine on the Left Bank. If you should wander into one of them, you would be likely to find men working at battered benches heaped with scores of gleaming chisels, some flat, some with curved blades, some wide, some narrow. You could watch them carve the leaves and rosettes on the top rail of a chair in the Louix XV style, plucking a chisel from the clutter on the bench to take a paper-thin curl from the wood, then dropping it to pick another which, to the untrained eye, looks no different from the first, as their forefathers had done back to the days of Louis XV.

Curiously enough, the output of shops that maintain a high level of workmanship, and faithfully copy the furniture of the eighteenth century, often costs more today than unsigned pieces made in the eighteenth and nineteenth centuries.

The purist, the collector who is interested only in authentic pieces with the name of the maker stamped into the wood at the time a piece was made, would disdain a $450 canapé, even one that was identical to a piece signed by a famous master and that might even have come from the same workshop. Chairs and sometimes even chests were made in pairs or sets and often only one of the pieces in a set was signed. If pieces have survived the years as a set

This is a late eighteenth-century Louis XVI provincial side chair, one of a set of four that sold for $300.

Provincial furniture made during the eighteenth century can be very attractive as well as modestly priced. This chair, one of a set of six, sold for $200.

and are identical, the unsigned pieces would take on some of the value of the signed piece, but would not command as high a price as the signed piece and the value as a set would therefore be reduced.

But if the pieces have become separated and turn up at different times and in different places, the signed piece could well bring several times the price of its identical mate. There have been instances where sets of identical eighteenth-century dining room chairs have been reassembled in New York over a long period of time and from many different sources, with each piece bringing a different price.

Wood tends to take on the coloring of antiquity in about fifty years. After that period, there is little difference in the appearance of raw wood. So even an expert examining the wood in a nineteenth-century chair and an identical chair from the eighteenth century would have difficulty in perceiving any difference. A piece that is unsigned, that is well-proportioned, and carefully worked cannot really be fixed in time beyond, say, the turn of the century. It is entirely possible that there were nineteenth-century carvers with as fine a hand and eye as those of the eighteenth century. It is also possible that a chair made in the eighteenth century which has not been subjected to abuse will show as little sign of wear as one made a hundred years later.

Something must be said here about instinct. A truly professional eye, looking at two apparently identical pieces, might well decide that one is eighteenth century, the other nineteenth. But it would be a judgment based on feeling and experience rather than on fact. Thus, I have come to the conclusion over the years that there is so little difference between a piece of furniture made in the eighteenth century and one made in the nineteenth century that, barring clear evidence to the contrary, any opinion as to which century a piece dates from is purely arbitrary and subject to disagreement, even among experts.

What is true of Louis XV, Louis XVI, and Empire furnishings is equally true of William and Mary, Queen Anne, the Georges I, II, and III, and Regency. What is different is how the craft evolved in Britain as compared to France. There was no revolution in eighteenth-century London, consequently no revulsion against eighteenth-century ruling-class taste.

Many fine English homes today are exactly as they were in the eighteenth century. An English housewife would never, at any

*This is probably a nineteenth-century copy of a
Louis XVI swivel desk chair. It sold for $400.*

time in history, have thought of emptying her rooms of Queen
Anne or Georgian furnishings in order to bring them up-to-date
with some current mode. She might have discarded her Eliza-
bethan pieces, but only because they were so heavy, gloomy, and
downright uncomfortable. But even in that case the chances are
the heavy oak furniture would have gone to a country house, or
into the servants' quarters. The change in such a case would have
been to Queen Anne, more than likely, or Georgian, with a scattering of French pieces, if she was a sophisticated English lady, if
only because they are so elegant and so graceful and certainly
comfortable.

The names we all know from eighteenth-century England are

This George II walnut wing armchair, dating from the second quarter of the eighteenth century, is a classic piece well worth the $3,750 it brought at auction. This is one style of chair that would sell for far less in contemporary reproduction because the only visible wood is the legs.

Chippendale, Adam, Sheraton, Hepplewhite, and, for the more sophisticated, William Vile, Thomas Johnson, Pierre Langlois, John Cobb, and William Ince, among others. The styles and periods are, as in France, the reigns of the kings and, in the case of Anne and Elizabeth, the queens. The periods most popular to this day are Queen Anne, the Georges I, II, and III, with a scattering of George IV, though much of the furniture of his period is called Regency because George IV served as Regent when George III became senile and could no longer exercise his authority.

That great period in English style which began in 1702 with

Queen Anne ran until 1830 when a new queen mounted the throne and ushered in the era in mores and decor that we know as Victorian.

There are few names remembered from the Queen Anne and earlier periods in furniture, and those that have come down to us are neither widely known nor of importance in the context of this volume. There was no real tradition in England for makers of case furniture or seat furniture to sign their pieces, although the practice was followed by some specialists—gilders and carvers in particular. Nor was there a guild to set down rules for furniture makers such as existed in France. Only in the working of precious metals were strict standards set governing the silver or gold content. Those standards required full identification of the owner, the branch of the guild to which he adhered, and the year in which the article was fashioned. Hallmarks punched into the metal tell the story to this day.

The need for strict controls to guarantee the value of the materials used did not exist in the case of furniture and there was only the tradition of pasting a trade label in a piece, few of which have survived. I own an eighteenth-century English piano which, in addition to the name and address of the maker, John Broadwood, and the year of the manufacture, which appear on the facia as would be the case with a modern Steinway, has inside the case a paper label written by hand with instructions in English and French for freeing hammers that stick. This kind of label has survived in a few instances on furniture, but generally only important pieces made for the ruling family and identified through the account books of the maker, or royal inventories of the period, can be definitely assigned to a particular workshop.

Stylistically, Queen Anne, whose brief reign from 1702 to 1714 gave her name to the period, was a bridge between the Georges and William and Mary, a rather heavy and often ornate style that borrowed important elements from the Dutch and French. The Queen Anne period gave birth to the Windsor chair which is reproduced to this day in the United States and England, and to the bonnet-top highboy. The period also produced impressive cabinetry in parts, not unlike the wall pieces made today in sections, except that these were sectioned from top to bottom, rather than from side to side.

This writer has in his barn (where it will surely become prey to worms) a magnificent three-piece Sheraton linen chest with two wide drawers and two shallow drawers in the bottom section, sliding shelf drawers in the middle section concealed behind tall doors of well-figured and inlaid mahogany, and a.top section with a broken-arch pediment. A splendid piece more than eight feet tall, it just does not fit in a house with seven-foot ceilings.

The mark of Queen Anne was simplicity. No gilt, little carving, smooth lines, elegance, and grace. The period produced graceful wing chairs with cabriole legs borrowed from the French, and pad feet; those engaging hall porter chairs that one still finds from time to time, with their enveloping hoods within which the hall porter could withdraw his miserable countenance from the gaze of his betters; the spoon-back chair, the horseshoe chair with its curved back and seat, the vase-shaped splat for dining room chairs, the claw-and-ball foot, which was enormously elaborated and strengthened in Chippendale's time and so is sometimes erroneously associated with his name as originator; the use of veneers in a pattern formed by woods of different colors and textures, a technique borrowed from the Dutch and greatly elaborated and refined later by the French; the card table—not our kind with folding legs to be stuffed behind the coats in the hall closet, but a graceful piece of furniture with a folding top and sometimes gate legs, with slides of wood or brass to hold candlesticks at the four corners to illuminate the play, with chess boards or backgammon boards inlaid on one of the surfaces. This is not by any means a complete list of all the forms furniture took in this most graceful period of English design. There were also the reading chair, with its triangular seat, on which the sitter faced the back with sometimes a bookrest suspended from it, the first cockfight chairs and a variety of stools and benches.

The names of the creators of these designs have been lost in the past. Not so the work of their successors.

Chippendale ensured that his name would persist—although this was surely not his objective—by publishing a book of drawings of furniture called *The Gentleman and Cabinet-Maker's Director*, which was widely circulated at the time. Three editions were published and the third edition, which appeared in 1762, has been reproduced and can be bought today in a good bookshop.*

There is little agreement among the experts as to where Chip-

---

The Gentleman and Cabinet-Maker's Director, by Thomas Chippendale. A reprint of the Third Edition, Dover Publications, Inc., New York, New York.

pendale's talents lay. Some say he was no more than a shrewd promoter and businessman whose best designs were the work of Robert Adam, whose stamp on architecture and interior design persists to this day. Others maintain that Chippendale was a talented designer in his own right. Many authorities believe that during his lifetime Chippendale absorbed and distilled five distinct styles—the ornate Palladian of George I, the French of the eighteenth century, Chinese, Gothic, and Adam—and put on each his own unmistakable touch.

He had, it is estimated, twenty journeymen cabinetmakers at work through the period when he flourished as a furniture maker in his shops in St. Martin's Lane, the center of cabinetmaking and a fashionable shopping district. He also is believed to have employed an equal number of apprentices. Many of these men left him to establish their own shops. Some emigrated to America, settling in Philadelphia, New York, and Baltimore, taking Chippendale's *Gentleman and Cabinet-Maker's Director* with them, and it is widely acknowledged that much of the fine cabinetry turned out in those cities in the eighteenth century came from the hands of men trained in his shops.

Since British cabinetmakers seldom signed their work, pieces that can be firmly attributed to Chippendale are extremely rare. Those that have been so identified are in Britain's stately homes—a writing table in Harewood House, for instance—and have been so identified by concise records preserved in the muniment rooms of the great English estates.

Nevertheless, pieces in the style attributed to Chippendale abound in copies made through the decades from the eighteenth century to the present time. Seldom does one find a piece that copies the designs in his book, since the drawings themselves often showed pieces with a variety of treatments, such as different legs or posts on his four-poster beds. Chippendale himself said in his book that the drawings were "so contrived that if no one drawing should singly answer the Gentleman's taste, there will yet be found a variety of hints, sufficient to construct a new one." Singularly enough, not one of the chairs is shown with the claw-and-ball foot which is regarded in the popular mind as the distinctive mark of Chippendale. Note well that the book was aimed at the "gentlemen" of the period, not the ladies, whose authority over the household did not extend to its furnishings.

The most distinctive of Chippendale innovations are chairs with delicately carved ribbon backs, the fretwork galleries and stretchers on tables in the Chinese taste and delicate ribbon moldings on the glass doors of breakfronts and other cabinets. He opened the splat on occasional and dining chairs, offering an infinite variety of styles for such backs, many of which have been copied through the centuries and can be bought new in superb and costly reproductions being made today.

Robert Adam drew his inspiration from classical Rome, where he studied architecture. Where Chippendale was lavish in the richness and intricacy of his designs, Adam leaned toward clean, formal lines. As architect to the king from 1762 on, he commissioned artists such as Angelica Kauffman to paint walls and ceilings of homes he designed for his patrons, as well as to decorate articles of furniture. A desk that reached the auction market in 1961 as part of the Harewood House Sale was designed by Adam and made by Chippendale. It brought $123,000. Today, it would probably bring $500,000. Most of Adam's designs for furniture were characterized by a classic architectural quality in which he often employed architectural details and the design motifs that he first saw in his studies of classical Rome.

Occasionally there appears on the market a demi-lune commode, probably made as a pair, forming a half circle and designed to rest against a wall, painted "in the manner of Angelica Kauffman" or veneered in satinwood with delicate marquetry, an Adam favorite. He designed many pieces in the French taste and some of his chairs might easily be mistaken for the product of the eighteenth-century Paris workshops.

Adam style persists to this day and was faithfully copied throughout the decades since he was active. Adam pieces inevitably bring high prices if they are of the period, and even later examples stimulate spirited bidding because of their desirability in today's more formal interiors.

George Hepplewhite is another controversial figure in the history of British furniture, the debate ranging all the way from a conviction that he maintained a shop in London and had the Prince of Wales as one of his clients, to the strongly argued belief by other authorities that no such person ever existed, and the designs attributed to him were the work of two anonymous cabinetmakers (Hepple and White?) who created the name. However, another authority insists that George Hepplewhite died in 1786 and his *Cabinet-Maker and Upholsterers Guide* was issued a year later under the name of G. Hepplewhite & Co., by his widow. The book was an instant success probably because its content was broader in scope than pattern books issued by Chippendale, and dealt with such mundane items as bedroom and dressing room pieces.

Whatever the facts, the style we know as Hepplewhite is clear and distinctive, characterized by great simplicity of line and great charm. Among his creations were the shield-back chair; the Prince of Wales back using the characteristic feathers in the splat; the urn-back chair and chair backs that use the anthemion (a flat, floral design), ears of wheat, and honeysuckle; as well as the oval back and circular back chair, with or without arms. The Hepplewhite sideboard and commode are pieces characterized by simple lines, square tapering legs, usually in mahogany but sometimes in lighter woods, closer to Adam in style than to Chippendale because of their clean lines.

As Hepplewhite pieces are generally small, they are particularly useful in today's homes. Copies have appeared ever since his day and continue to appear, and at auction or in antique shops they are much sought after.

There is less confusion about Thomas Sheraton, but only slightly less, and frequently authorities on the period avoid getting into the controversial question of who and what Sheraton was. The consensus seems to be that Sheraton was a preacher who arrived in London from his native Stockton-on-Tees, in 1791, armed with an assortment of religious tracts and his book of furniture designs which he promptly published under the title *Cabinet-Maker and Upholsterer's Drawing Book*. It was published in four parts between 1791 and 1794 with 113 designs. The book was such a success that he later published the *Cabinet Dictionary* and *The Cabinet-Maker, Upholsterer and General Artist's Encyclopedia*, which appeared in 1805, labeled Part I. Part II was never published. After Sheraton's death in 1806, a posthumous work appeared entitled *Designs for Household Furniture*.

There is serious question as to whether Sheraton ever made furniture, and nowhere does one find any explanation of the dichotomy between cabinetry and religion that he seems to have melded successfully. One of his critics has charged that all he had for sale in "the squalid shop in the dingy back street . . . was . . . books, stationery and sermons."

Whatever the facts it must be said that, like Hepplewhite,

Sheraton furniture exists, has a distinctive style, and is much in demand to this day.

There were other design books issued in London during the eighteenth-century by architects, builders, and cabinetmakers. Thomas Johnson, a carver, published a series of engravings of various designs for carving decorative items, following these with a book called *One Hundred and Fifty New Designs*. The cabinetry firm of Ince and Mayhew published *The Universal System of Household Furniture* in the third quarter of the eighteenth century. If neither of these names is familiar it is probably because they designed in the rococo style that was popular in the early part of the century and is regarded today as too florid for most tastes.

What gives all this importance, from our point of view, is that furniture in the styles we know by the more popular names of Chippendale, Hepplewhite, Sheraton, and the earlier Queen Anne has been turned out over the years in vast quantities, most of it well made and serviceable, and is liberally available today at a scale of prices that rises with each piece's age, but in a range broad enough to fit into our purposes in this volume.

Whether or not any individual piece can be attributed to the hand or even the workshop of the designer, the finest workmanship of the period when the designers flourished comes high. But for our purposes a nineteenth-century copy is quite acceptable.

A number of British and American firms are making furniture today in the styles of eighteenth-century England. It is of excellent quality and workmanship and often costs more than we would have to pay for an earlier version at auction or in some antique shops.

There are, of course, many other styles of furnishings—Dutch, for instance, characterized in the case of the eighteenth-century furniture by rich (overly so, to some tastes) floral marquetry inlays, a kind of workmanship in which the Dutch early became expert, and fine dark mahogany furniture made of wood brought back in the holds of Dutch sailing vessels from the islands of the East and West Indies.

Italian furniture that you are likely to encounter in antique shops or at auction sales in this country is either Venetian or Florentine. You may find painted chair frames and cabinetry in a lovely ivory or faded green and gold, or heavy seventeenth-century, and earlier, chests and refectory tables of massive proportions, richly carved in dark woods. The big chests, generally with two small drawers at the top and two doors exposing a shelf below, are often used today to hold liquor bottles and glasses, the tops serving admirably as bars.

Then there is the whole of Middle Europe, the countries we know as Germany, Austria, Poland, Czechoslovakia, and the Balkans which, in the eighteenth century, were a myriad of little principalities, duchies, and kingdoms, each with its ruler and its court and the stately homes of its lesser nobility—its grafs and its barons, its protectors and its church dignitaries—resplendent in their furs and satins, in baroque architectural settings, surrounded by heavily ornate baroque and rococo furnishings. You can still see them today in the carefully preserved monuments that escaped the ravages of World War II, particularly in Bavaria where King Ludwig, called the Mad King, sought to re-create Versailles in the rolling woodlands of the South German state he once ruled. The furniture of the eighteenth century in Germany ranged from baroque in the early part of the century, through rococo and ended in an attractive neoclassicism. There were many outside influences evident, in particular the taste of the English and Dutch. Craftsmanship was superior. (It must be remembered that some of the finest French cabinetmakers came out of German backgrounds.)

Then there is Biedermeier, a style that developed in the early nineteenth century and which bore, unfortunately, the name of an Austrian comic-strip character who was representative in the popular mind of everything middle class and bad taste. Actually, Biedermeier is rather more functional than other styles of the period and pieces that would fit this description would also fit well in today's homes.

Of all these styles, it is Italian furniture that is most sought after in this country today, both the painted pieces of the Venetian littoral and the heavy carved chests and tables meant for the dining halls of stone castles. But the prices may be high, particularly since Italian buyers have been combing the American market for such pieces and repatriating them as fast as they are found.

CHAPTER

10

BUYING FINE ART WITH CONFIDENCE

A PAINTING is a unique item. Whatever its quality, whoever the
artist, it represents the distillation of one precise segment of his in-
tellect, one precise stage in the development of his talent or genius,
as well as of his knowledge of his medium and the techniques involved in its application.

It is almost impossible to equate one painting, in terms of monetary value, with another by the same artist. He may do a dozen
paintings of a single scene, as Monet did with the lily ponds at
Giverny, the cathedral at Chartres and the rows of poplars along
France's canals. No two paintings he did of each of those subjects
are alike. Indeed, he would not have been capable, even if he had
wanted to, of painting two alike.

The market puts a different value on each painting of such a
series, as does critical judgment of aesthetic value. Each critic, in
the final essence, appraises the artist's success in treating his subject
in each version of the same subject. Some of the paintings of the
lily pond series may be considered failures by comparison with
others that have a lush, dreamlike quality. Monet, writing of the
task he had set himself with the water lilies, said to Gustave
Geffroy in a letter in 1890: "I have gone back to some things that
can't possibly be done; water, with weeds waving at the bottom. It
is a wonderful sight, but it drives one crazy to try to paint it. But
that is the kind of thing I am always tackling."

His worst failures Monet destroyed with his palette knife,
slashing the canvas to ribbons in his despair at his inability to
achieve the effect he sought. Such is the importance of names
today that, had Monet's failures escaped the knife, had they been
permitted to survive, they would be traded in the auction rooms
and the galleries of important dealers today for many thousands of

dollars. And there would be aesthetic justification for their sale, since even the failures of a great artist say something about his development and his struggle with his subject.

Not all artists destroyed their failures. In every studio of a serious artist one is likely to find stacked against the wall dust-covered canvases which represent such failures, some of them finished works that the artist does not consider worthy of his name, some of them experiments that reflected a deviation from the mainstream of his work and had brought the artist to a dead end, some of them mere sketches. Others possibly were abandoned because the artist lost interest in the subject or saw no purpose to be served from further scraping and laying on of paint.

They remain there, ignored, often until the artist's death, unsigned, undated, the very subject matter sometimes forgotten. Then the heirs and trustees of the estate, or his dealer, arrange an atelier sale. Everything his brush touched is dusted off, framed, stamped as evidence that it came from his studio, and sold, often with a certificate from his widow or a child attesting to the fact that it is by the artist's hand.

In his last years Renoir was no longer able to hold a brush in his hand. But such was his drive that he worked with a paint brush tied to his wrist and fingers. Some of these paintings have survived and are no more than a travesty of his earlier genius. But the magic of the Renoir name always finds them a market at a good price.

A friend of mine once went to look at the collection of a famous New York magazine publisher. When asked later what it consisted of, he replied:

"Third-rate paintings by first-rate artists, second-rate paintings by second-rate artists, and first-rate paintings by third-rate artists."

He was rating the artists by the taste of the times—the mid-1950s when the vogue was for Impressionist and Post-Impressionist painters and a handful of old masters. Given your choice, which would you prefer? A third-rate painting by a first-rate artist or a first-rate painting by a third-rate artist? A Renoir from his failing years or a brilliantly executed canvas of an allegorical scene by Rosa Bonheur?

Rosa Bonheur was a French painter of the middle nineteenth century, a follower and contemporary of Landseer. In 1887 a painting of hers entitled "Frightened Herd," all lolling tongues, goring horns and blood, brought a reputed $380,000—the equivalent, in today's inflated dollars, to the best of Renoir. A few years ago the picture turned up at a London auction and sold for $2,000.

Better documented is the price paid by the senior Morgan, Junius Spencer Morgan, in 1886 for Bonheur's "Horse Fair" now owned by the Metropolitan Museum. It was $60,000, the equivalent in today's dollars of $268,000. The highest price reached by one of her pictures in recent years was $3,000. Now interest in the nineteenth century is increasing, and her work is making an impressive comeback.

Or consider Adolphe William Bouguereau, another nineteenth-century French painter, this time a devotee of allegory. In 1886 a huge painting of a centaur seizing a beauteous maiden with a dimpled belly and luscious breasts, while striking a murderous blow at her bare-buttocked swain, brought $146,000. It sold in 1960 for $250.

Were Bonheur and Bouguereau considered first rate in the nineteenth century? Indeed they were. Bonheur was a celebrated figure in France. In 1868 she drove Millais, another French painter, in a hansom cab from Fontainebleau Station dressed, in anticipation of twentieth-century surrealism, as a priest and wearing the sash of the French Legion of Honor.

And what about Monet, whose 1874 painting, "Impression-Sunrise," gave a name to a whole school of painting, who wrote to Georges Charpentier, the publisher and collector in 1878:

"I am literally penniless here, obliged to petition people, almost to beg for my keep, not having a penny to buy canvas and paints. . . . I will send you a painting I think you will like. I ask you 150 francs for it, or, if that price seems too high, 100 francs. . . . If the picture is not what you want, I will change it for another when I come back."

Or Renoir, who wrote to Charpentier in 1877:

"May I ask you, if it is within possibility, the sum of three hundred francs . . . ?"

A painting of Mme. Charpentier and her children hangs in the Metropolitan Museum of Art, which bought it for 50,000 francs from Charpentier while Renoir was still alive. Asked what he had paid for it, Charpentier replied: "Three hundred francs and a lunch."

Were Monet and Renoir considered first-rate painters at the time when they were at the height of their genius? On the contrary. In a period when the Bonheurs and Bouguereaus of the world were selling their paintings for substantial sums, the Monets

Renoir's portrait, "Mme. Charpentier and Her Children," now at the Metropolitan Museum of Art. When Charpentier, a Paris art dealer, was asked what he had paid for it, he replied, "Three hundred francs and a luncheon." M. Charpentier later sold the painting to the Metropolitan for $50,000.

and the Renoirs were being laughed out of the Paris exhibitions and were begging their patrons for paltry sums to buy bread, canvas, and paint.

In today's world, anything they touched a hand to has taken on a value they would have considered impossible.

To take one contemporary example of foresight, Ludwig Bemelmans, the writer and illustrator best known for his children's books, once had a dealer who bribed the janitor of the building where the artist had his studio to remove from Bemelman's wastebasket every scrap of paper on which his crayons or brushes had made a mark and many of these pieces were later sold as sketches.

Bemelmans, after all, had a certain facility and selling the contents of his wastebaskets is not the worst crime committed in the name of art.

Modern marketing methods have created such a demand for paintings that buyers for chains of galleries and art departments of discount stores now comb the attics of Paris and other cities buying up everything with paint on it, almost without regard for quality.

We are a nation of faddists and the merchandising of culture in the past few years has created a boom in Art with a capital A. A whole new industry has been created to meet the demand, making and selling miserable daubs whose principal appeal is that they are "original" or "genuine" oil paintings.

They are made in a variety of ways. A strip of canvas is unrolled along the length of a warehouse wall and artists attack it, using assembly-line methods. One may rough in a series of scenes or one continuous scene. Others may follow him, one painting in the reds, another the blues and so on. The finished canvas is dried by heat and cut apart in frame-size morsels, stretched, mounted, and encased in molded plastic frames, ready for the market.

They are being sold everywhere. In smaller communities they may be offered in a shop that makes a pretense of being a legitimate gallery, conducting a framing business on the side. In the big cities, the technique is that of the bankruptcy or fire sale, with big, garish signs proclaiming "sensational values" in "genuine oil paintings" for $25 to $300 or more. They exploit the legitimate hunger of a whole segment of our society for a touch of color and beauty in otherwise drab lives. For betraying this hunger, for feeding this need with trash if for no other reason, they are beyond contempt.

A cut above this method is one where an artist sets up a dozen or a hundred canvases on stretchers around a room with the same picture roughed in, often that of a roguish-eyed miss displaying a touch of bosom, and goes from one to the next with a palette of paint putting in the same color in the same places on each of the canvases until he has a series of more or less identical works. This is a form of mass production only slightly less deserving of contempt.

An artist needs a sense of perspective. So does the buyer of a painting. The purpose of all this is to give you a sense of perspective in deciding what kind of art you will hang on the walls of your home. Between the great names of the Impressionist and Post-Impressionist period, and the miserable, mass-produced assembly-line product, the $250 daubs in their plastic frames, there lies a whole world of legitimate art—posters, prints, drawings, water-colors, gouaches, collages, primitives, old masters, young artists, not to mention the whole other world of decorative objects that can go on the walls, into which you can dip almost at will and at often very modest cost, to beautify your home with legitimate works of art or craftsmanship.

The more we know about fine art the less likely we are to be terrified at the thought of coming to grips with it. Even the language of art puts some people in awe.

Let us take the category "old masters." Awe-inspiring, isn't it? "Where do I get off, little old me," one might say, "living in a split-level ranch on a quarter acre in Hastings, New York, to be thinking of buying an old master painting to hang on the wall of my living room?"

Well, why not, if I find one I like at a price I can afford?

Let us look at what an old master really is. First of all, of course, it is old. And in the purist definition of the term, it is from the hand of a master. Webster says an old master, in the personal sense, is "1. A superior artist or craftsman of established reputation, especially a distinguished painter of the 16th, 17th, or early 18th Century." And, in the impersonal sense, "2. a work by an old master."

Note the words "established reputation" and "distinguished painter." They befit the precise, true definition. But in the terms accepted today, when we speak of an old master painting, we use the term as defining a whole period of art and include any painting of that period—roughly prior to the eighteenth century, back to the Gothic primitives of religious art which might more properly be referred to as medieval or renaissance art.

The old master sales catalogues of the great auction houses of the world would be thin indeed if all they contained were works by "distinguished painters" of "established reputation," since many of the paintings included in such sales are by unknowns.

The fact is that the distinguished and reputable old masters worked often in large studios. They had students and followers who worked with them. Often they drew a composition on board or canvas, painted the critical features such as the heads and hands of the personages in the painting, then left it to others to fill in the details of robes and background, using the knowledge they had gained from the master.

The followers and students of such masters at the same time were engaged on their own works, painting their own compositions, often emulating the style of the master with great precision, often producing a work that might catch his eye, to which he might put his own brush to correct a line or improve a texture and thus leave his indelible imprint to confuse the art historians of the future. As a result, the study of old master paintings, whose attribution is in doubt, has become an important pursuit for academics and experts alike.

Then along came generation after generation of copyists, artists who made their livings sitting in one spot in a museum before one painting which they would reproduce with meticulous detail, brush stroke by brush stroke, employing the same techniques and materials as those used by the masters of the originals. Their copies may not, in the first instance, have been sold as forgeries but later were passed off as originals. I recall a Giorgione which hung on the wall of a small salon in a Paris apartment I once rented, which bore on its reverse a gobbet of sealing wax in which was impressed a seal certifying that it was a "true copy" of the original.

Signatures are of little help. Until the eighteenth century, paintings were seldom signed. Painters were often rather naïve about the lasting value of their work and their names. There are recorded instances involving Boucher, the eighteenth-century French master of cherubs and discreetly unveiled maidens, and Corot, the nineteenth-century French landscape painter, who were so flattered when students produced paintings precisely in their style that they signed them so the students could sell them for more than their own names would merit.

Corot has been widely subjected to imitation and forgery, and there have been estimates that whereas he produced possibly seven hundred pictures of his own during his lifetime, there are upward of ten thousand Corots in the United States alone. Other painters whose work has been widely copied and sold with forged signatures are Rousseau, the French primitive, and Utrillo, the twentieth-century painter of Montmartre and country village streets. These are names to be wary of.

Not so long ago I was asked to look at some pictures that had been bought by a young man with more money than caution, two of which were, I was told, Utrillos. I stopped in the doorway of his living room, turned to the man, and asked: "Did you pay very much for these pictures?" "Enough," he replied.

"Get your money back, if you can," I said. "They are fakes."

"But you haven't even looked at them," he said. "How can you tell from this distance?"

I marched across the room, took down the painting hung over his fireplace and turned so the back faced him.

"Look at the canvas," I said. "Does it look new?"

He nodded.

"Utrillo has been dead for twenty years," I said. "In twenty years canvas would begin to show signs of age." When I looked at the back of the canvas, it was obvious it had been cut from a roll not more than a few months earlier.

The problem of attribution is a complex one. In some cases part of a painting may definitely be attributed to one of the great masters by the details of brush strokes, or by the delicate rendering of a characteristic pair of eyes, or of the mouth, or by the way the hands are painted, the strength or grace of a gesture or a posture. Sometimes there may be an obscure documentary reference in ancient archives that describes a specific painting executed for a particular person by a great master. Such a record may be useful as evidence of the existence of a painting, but still not conclusive. A historian studying a particular work must decide for himself whether the evidences of the master's hand are strong enough to warrant an attribution to him, and must be able to support his attribution with outside evidence or convincing reason.

More often than one might expect, it happens that a piece of sculpture or a painting bought for a few hundred dollars is shown, on the basis of painstaking research, to be the work of a great master, worth a fortune. There are many recent instances in point.

A couple of years ago Ira Spanierman, a young art dealer whose father operated one of the important secondary auction houses in New York City, bought a portrait for $325 at Sotheby Parke Bernet.

The picture had been consigned by the widow of a New York collector who had shown it to a number of dealers and galleries and had been assured that it was worth no more than several hundred dollars. The auction house catalogued it as a portrait of Francis I of Spain by an unknown Italian-school artist.

Spanierman, whose eye had been sharpened from childhood by constant exposure to arrangements of paint on panel and canvas of all schools and all qualities, was not satisfied with those opinions

"Their Just Deserves" by Sir John Gilbert,
British, 1817–97, 35½ by 27½ inches, $900.

Nineteenth-century European paintings are not only highly dec-
orative, in almost any kind of setting, they also continue to be
a "best buy," even though their prices are constantly rising. A
vast proportion of such paintings sold at auction these days still
bring under $1,000. Here and on the following pages are some
examples from a recent sale in New York.

"Fishing Vessels Offshore" by Christiaan Cornelis Kannemans,
Dutch, 1812–84, 12 by 17½ inches, $800.

and made his own study. Months later he announced that the
painting was a long lost portrait by Raphael of Lorenzo de Medici,
an attribution that was fully supported by an article in *The
Burlington*, a scholarly London magazine of great prestige. The article recited the history of the painting and accepted it without
question as the original portrait by Raphael.

The painting was in the inventory of the Medicis from 1553
until 1783. From that year, for a period of roughly seventy-five
years, there is a gap in its history. It was then reported in the
collection of Hollingworth Magniac of Colworth Hall, England,
whose records listed the painting in the nineteenth century. In
1962 the painting turned up at a sale at Christie, Manson and
Woods auction galleries at London, catalogued at that time as
"perhaps the best of a number of copies of a lost Raphael." It was

"Arabs Playing Checkers" by Gustavo Simoni,
an Italian born in 1846, 30 by 21 inches, $800.

"*A Flock of Sheep Beside a Cottage*" *by Edward Charles Williams,*
British, 1839–89, 11 by 9 inches, $400.

bought by an Atlantic City, New Jersey, dealer who subsequently
sold it to the New York collector.

It would be difficult to put a value on a Raphael of this importance, but certainly $2.5 million would not be excessive. Spanier-
man has thus far refused all offers for the picture.

*"A Shepherd Tending His Flock," attributed to Franz De Beul,
Belgian, nineteenth century, 24 by 32 inches, $600.*

*"The Hour of Devotion" by Hans Hamza,
German, born 1850, 7½ by 5½ inches, $800.*

"Playful Puppies" by Henrietta Ronner, Dutch, 1821–1909, 9¾ by 7¾ inches, $400.

"The Pipe Smoker" by W. Roessler, German, 9¼ by 7 inches, $225.

Spanierman's discovery followed one by another New York art dealer, Julius H. Weitzner, who paid $6,410, a not inconsiderable sum to venture on a gamble, for a painting at a country auction in England which was identified only as "of the Siennese school, 15th Century." The picture later was identified as a work by Duccio, the great Trecento (fourteenth century) Siennese master. The British Government paid Weitzner $360,000 to buy the work for London's National Gallery. The fact that the Duccio was the focus of a scandal involving the operations of an auction ring does not detract from the importance of Weitzner's discovery.

The Metropolitan Museum of Art paid $225 at another Sotheby Parke Bernet auction for an engaging piece of stucco statuary catalogued as a "polychromed stucco bust of a young woman holding flowers, after Verrocchio." A few days later the little statue was on the front page of the New York *Times*. Edward Fowles, former owner of the Duveen Galleries, said the piece was the work of Verrocchio himself, or perhaps that of Leonardo da Vinci, worth at least $500,000. He said he had bought the statue in Europe acting as agent for Duveen for $50,000, and that Duveen had later sold it to Mrs. Hamilton Rice. The statue is almost identical to a marble in the Bargello Museum in Florence called "The Lady with the Primroses." The Florence museum attributes that piece to Verrocchio.

Months later the Metropolitan Museum published the results of a study in which it attributed the Bargello marble to Leonardo, and said the stucco it had bought was a cast made from the marble. Whether the cast was made in 1915, just before it was bought by Mr. Fowles, or in 1515, while Leonardo was still alive, would bear importantly on its value. A study by the Museum's John Goldsmith Phillips offers evidence that it dates from circa 1475.

This may not be the end of the story on any of those works. Later evidence dug up by tomorrow's art historians may further strengthen the attributions, or even change them completely. The cast made from the Bargello marble has been owned by the Metropolitan for a decade but has only been exhibited once briefly in that time. While it still puts the date at 1475, the attribution has again been changed to "workshop of Verrocchio."

The possibility of finding and identifying a work by one of the great masters is one of the factors that keep the wheels turning in the market for old masters, that brings dealers and experts to the presale exhibitions to study pictures through magnifying glasses and search their memories and research materials for clues pointing to a painting's origins. To those who deal in old masters it is a game far more fascinating than roulette, a kind of Russian roulette without the threat of death.

None of this is intended to titillate you or to raise your hopes of finding a lost masterpiece. On the contrary, it is intended to reassure you, to tell you that the best of us make mistakes. Hundreds of pictures by artists of past centuries are sold every year for a few hundred dollars. If you see one you like and can buy it for $300 or $500, take it home and live with it for a while. When you can afford to do so, have it cleaned and, if need be, restored. It might cost you as much again as the picture itself, but one never knows what might be revealed under centuries of dirt and layers of brown varnish and overpainting. A good restorer can repair a torn canvas in many cases and can pull together a picture on panel that has dried out and split, often so skillfully that a crack is no longer visible.

You will be surprised at the number of paintings that sell for under $500. Whatever the attribution, they generally come from the hand of one artist, working out the problems of his medium and his composition. And so they are valid works of art, not to be compared with the "genuine oil paintings" of the assembly-line trade. At the very least you may acquire a fine antique frame that could be worth as much as you paid for the picture. There is a lively trade in antique frames and often pictures are bought and discarded, or reframed and sold again, the original frames being restored to be sold to collectors looking for an appropriate frame for a painting, or to hold mirrors.

When we move on through the eighteenth and nineteenth centuries, the confusion about attributions is often further complicated by a new element—signatures. Instead of simplifying matters, as one might imagine would be the case, signatures often serve only to add to the confusion.

Take the case, for instance, of François Boucher, the eighteenth-century French artist whose deplorable habits with regard to the use of his name have been mentioned earlier. Just recently this writer saw a lovely painting in a Long Island antique shop of three cupids in a parklike setting, at what must have been intended as the end of a light summer shower, for the central cupid is lifting a cape under which the three had apparently been sheltered. It is signed in gray paint "Boucher" and indistinctly dated, possibly

1764. Boucher died in 1770, so the date is right. The signature, too, appears to be in a style used by the artist.

The painting also seems right. There is a combination of childish grace and strength about the figures that was characteristic of the artist. The colors are good, the bosky setting typical, the age cracks in the varnish look legitimate. Yet, knowing a little about the painter's history, I would hesitate to pay $3,000 for the painting, let alone the $30,000 that was asked. The reason is that Boucher operated a large studio in which were produced drawings, paintings, designs for porcelain and wall coverings, as well as cartoons for tapestries and other fabrics—operated, in short, as would a contemporary design studio, prepared to take on any commission from portraiture to murals to dainty reserve paintings for Sèvres teacups. To further compound the problem, Boucher was lavish in the use of his signature, sometimes even when that was the only point where his hand touched the work. There was, further, a revival of his style in the nineteenth century and works in the manner of Boucher—which this painting probably was—abound.

From the nineteenth century there is a wealth of pictures in which the artists portrayed the life around them, often the life of simple peasants in their kitchens and farmyards, going about their pursuits and their pleasures. These are called "genre" paintings and until recently, at least, they had no great popularity in our times. Now they attract interest and prices are rising.

This has been true, also, of Victorian paintings, and especially of the pre-Raphaelites, a group of mainly English artists who sought to revive the style and even the subject matter of the period before Raphael, which means the early sixteenth century. They were highly accomplished artists, whose prices have also risen and will probably continue to do so.

Nineteenth-century Dutch landscape and seascape paintings are also enjoying a revival, but here again there are many obscure artists whose work can be bought for less than $500. One of the sensations of recent auction sales has been the rise in prices for paintings by members of the Koekkoek family, Dutch artists of the nineteenth century, a large family all of whose male members apparently took to the brush. Some of the Koekkoeks are quite highly regarded, their paintings of harbor scenes and landscapes often bringing in the neighborhood of $15,000–$20,000. Others, however, often sell for a few hundred dollars.

Nineteenth-century paintings will often be found at auction

sales in this country, as well as in antique shops and picture galleries. Before shopping for genre paintings it would be well to attend a few auctions, where such paintings come up to gain some measure of what they bring and to serve as a guide when you come upon something you like in a gallery.

This brings us to the period of greatest interest to most of us today—the art of the last hundred years, starting with the birth of Impressionism. It is quite true that the work of the major Impressionist artists are beyond reach of all except the very rich and the well-endowed museums. It is also true, unfortunately, that the work of the whole vast group of lesser painters of the Impressionist school have now risen to the point where their most important works, oil paintings on canvas, would be out of reach of most people today. But there is more to the story than that.

Impressionism marked the emergence of painting from the rigid rules of the academy and the studio into the bright sunshine and open air. It was a process that affected many painters directly and many others indirectly, opening the way to experimentation in materials and techniques that would have been impossible had not Impressionism made the break with the academic tradition.

The great painters of the Impressionist period are very much with us. We know them well—Monet, Manet, Cézanne. Renoir, Van Gogh, and so on. The same is true of the painters who followed them—Picasso, Matisse, Toulouse-Lautrec, Utrillo, Vlaminck.

But what about Paul Serusier and Georges Mathieu, Michael Kikoine and Claude Venard—all painters of the last hundred years —whose works hang in museums and are regularly sold at auction? While their oil paintings have now reached levels where they would no longer qualify as possibilities for the budget collector, their watercolors, gouaches and drawings may still be within reach, as are their prints.

Again it must be emphasized that whatever you buy, a degree of caution must be exercised. We all know of the great fakes and forgeries of recent years, by disillusioned painters who were unable to sell pictures bearing their own names and so resorted to painting in the more salable styles of their illustrious predecessors. Forgeries and fakes of most of the great names exist, right down to drawings in their styles. Doubtless the lesser painters have similarly been imitated. But forgers of modern art tended to work in areas where the payoff would be more likely to justify the exercise.

The best advice is to use caution, particularly if you are planning to spend any considerable sum on a picture. If you are not certain of what you are getting, spend a little more and obtain the advice of a dealer knowledgeable in the work of the artist or at least of his period. A dealer will often go to an auction exhibition with you and give you his opinion and will even bid for you for a modest percentage of the price you pay. If you have any doubt, that modest percentage can be money well spent.

THE VAST RANGE OF AMERICANA

Enough about the art and artisans of Europe. It is time now to deal with the area of greatest and growing interest in this country —Americana, another of those broad and amorphous terms that takes in a lot of territory. It includes everything from the paintings of John Singleton Copley and Benjamin West to Indian relics and the crudest household implements of pioneers.

Anyone who is even remotely interested in art and antiques knows that the past few years have seen an enormous rise in the value of Americana—furniture, paintings, objects of all kinds, right up to depression glass (which was handed out free at movie houses), barbed wire (which appears to have been made in a wide variety of forms, sufficient to warrant books on the subject), and all other areas known as "collectibles."

American furniture of quality came from the port cities of the East, from Virginia north to Massachusetts. This was where the latest examples of English furniture and the latest books on English design arrived with each shipload of emigrants from the mother country, among them the craftsmen from the workshops around London's St. Martin's Lane who became the major American cabinetmakers.

It is small wonder, then, that the finest American workmanship followed styles laid down by the creative British designers. There is American William and Mary furniture, with its highboys standing on turned legs and stretchers that are also used on tables and chairs. There is American Queen Anne furniture with all the grace and delicacy of its English counterpart but with an added strength and simplicity. And there are American Chippendale, Sheraton, and Hepplewhite, as well as the distinctly American Duncan

*This block-front, slant-lid desk in mahogany, with a fan-
carving on the door at center, sold for $2,100.*

Phyfe, which coincided with the classical revival in early nineteenth-century England and France.

The periods of American furniture lag behind the same periods
in England by as much as a quarter of a century or more. The first
Queen Anne furniture was made in America in about 1725 and
the style enjoyed vogue until roughly 1750, whereas in England
the Queen Anne period ended in roughly 1714. American Chippendale furniture was being turned out in Philadelphia, Baltimore,
and New York as late as the 1790s, whereas the Chippendale period in England is regarded as having come to a close, for authentic
pieces of the period, by 1779.

None of this is to be taken to mean that furniture of those styles
and periods was made only during those years. As we have shown,

Fine cabinetry in valuable woods such as walnut and mahogany always commands higher prices. This American Queen Anne walnut chest on frame, made in Pennsylvania and standing six feet high, sold for $4,200. Occasionally such pieces do turn up at more modest prices.

all popular styles were being produced decade after decade through the nineteenth century and are still being turned out today.

The reason for the time lag had its base in economics and communications. During the early decades of the eighteenth century the American economy was just beginning the dynamic growth that continues today, with the emergence of a rich merchant, shipping, and landowner class whose tastes were those of the rich of England.

Some of their homes survive and have been restored to their eighteenth-century elegance either by the present owners or as historic monuments. Their style and decor is in the English tradition, their furnishings made by craftsmen lately arrived from England, some in walnut but more often in mahogany, which replaced the

A fine Chippendale American curly-maple, slant-lid desk dating from the eighteenth century. It sold for $2,200.

An American eighteenth-century Queen Anne maple drop-leaf table with cabriole legs and pad feet, a splendid piece for $850.

simple, often crude pieces in maple, pine, and other soft woods, made by less gifted craftsmen.

The most important names in eighteenth-century American cabinetry and the cities in which those craftsmen worked are:

Thomas Affleck, Philadelphia, Pennsylvania
Nehemiah Adams, Salem, Massachusetts
Michael Allison, New York, New York
Elbert Anderson, New York, New York
Stephen Badlam, Dorchester Lower Mills, Massachusetts
Nathaniel Bowen, Marblehead, Massachusetts
Aaron Chapin, Hartford, Connecticut
Eliphalet Chapin, East Windsor, Connecticut
John Cogswell, Boston, Massachusetts

Job Coit, Jr., Boston, Massachusetts
Henry Connelly, Philadelphia, Pennsylvania
John Davey, Philadelphia, Pennsylvania
Nicholas Disbrowe, Hartford, Connecticut
The Dunlap Family, New Hampshire
Edward Evans, Philadelphia, Pennsylvania
John Folwell, Philadelphia, Pennsylvania
Benjamin Frothingham, Charlestown, Massachusetts
John Gaines, Portsmouth, New Hampshire
Parnell Gibbs, Philadelphia, Pennsylvania
John Goddard & Family, Newport, Rhode Island
Jonathan Gostelowe, Philadelphia, Pennsylvania
Ephraim Haines, Philadelphia, Pennsylvania
John Harrison, Philadelphia, Pennsylvania
William Hook, Salem, Massachusetts
Edmund Johnson, Salem, Massachusetts
Charles Honore Lannier, New York, New York
William Lemmon, Salem, Massachusetts
Samuel McIntire, Salem, Massachusetts
Duncan Phyfe, New York, New York
Benjamin Randolph, Philadelphia, Pennsylvania
Aaron Roberts, New Britain, Connecticut
Elijah & Jacob Sanderson, Salem, Massachusetts
William Savery, Philadelphia, Pennsylvania
John Seymour, Boston, Massachusetts
John Shaw, Annapolis, Maryland
Jonathan Shoemaker, Philadelphia, Pennsylvania
John & Simeon Skillin, Boston, Massachusetts
Edmund & Job Townsend, Newport, Rhode Island
Holmes Weaver, Newport, Rhode Island

These are not, by any means, the only cabinetmakers who flourished in the coastal centers of the raw country during the eighteenth century. But they are the principal ones whose names have come down to us, either through their records, the records kept by the families who patronized them, or from their trade labels pasted inside drawers or under chair rails.

WILLIAM DOYLE GALLERIES, INC.

Duncan Phyfe tub-back chair, originally the property of Henry Brevoort, who built the Fifth Avenue mansion that later became the famous Brevoort Hotel. The chair was sold at William Doyle Gallery for a record $22,000. This is a style that has been reproduced continuously since the early nineteenth century.

These are the men who produced the exquisite Chippendale, Sheraton, Queen Anne, and Hepplewhite pieces, many of which are superior in design and at least equal in craftsmanship to the English originals, as well as the later fine Federal furniture. A large number of these pieces have come down to us intact—a surprising number. Many of them are in museums or historical mansions or in the homes of descendants of the families for which they were made. There are still important collections and pieces in old homes on Long Island, in New England, Pennsylvania, and indeed all up and down the East Coast.

These cabinetmakers created the block-front chests and desks,

A cherrywood tall case clock made by James Robinson, Williamston, Massachusetts, which brought $1,600 at auction. To its left is a rare Federal inlaid mahogany "Dish Dial" shelf clock made by Aaron Willard in Boston in 1800–10.

the highboy and the lowboy, distinctive Queen Anne and Chippendale pieces including the great Philadelphia armchairs of that period. They constructed the bonnet-top highboy with its elaborate finials and shell carvings, the Duncan Phyfe pieces with their roots in Sheraton and borrowings from the French Empire, the graceful sofas and settees with their elegantly splayed legs, the characteristic Duncan Phyfe side tables and dining tables, the two- and three-part dining tables, the lyre-back chairs and side tables with lyre supports, all traditionally American, though they owe substantial debt to European precursors.

Through the generations since the preceding list of craftsmen flourished, their designs have been copied and reproduced and it is often difficult even for an expert to tell whether a Duncan Phyfe piece is an original, from his workshop in New York City, or a copy made later in the nineteenth or twentieth century. Which-

The summer kitchen of Woolfolk House in Virginia, before it was dismantled for a house sale, containing eighteenth- and nineteenth-century furniture and implements.

ever it is, furniture of this kind has always been of quality and whether it is original or not, if the price is right, such pieces are desirable for any home.

Since authentic pieces of fine American furniture by the great eighteenth-century cabinetmakers are much in demand by museums and collectors, they are likely to bring prices several times as high as the English pieces that inspired them. A recent instance demonstrates just how wide the price differential can be.

Recently an English collector brought a set of five chairs in to Sotheby's in London which he had bought at a country auction in England during the 1920s. Jonathan Bourne a Sotheby expert, considered them of English origin and set a value on them of $8,000–10,000, as examples of George II workmanship with exceptionally well-carved feet done in hairy-paw style. But certain stylistic inconsistencies and peculiar structural features troubled Mr. Bourne and he sent a photograph of one of the chairs to Ronald De Silva, then the American furniture expert at Sotheby Parke Bernet in New York. To Mr. De Silva, the chairs appeared to be identical with a famous "sample" chair in the Stamper-Blackwell parlor of the H. F. du Pont Winterthur Museum, and he asked that the chairs be shipped to New York.

Examining them closely Mr. De Silva found that point-for-point they matched the Winterthur chair. Then he stripped off one of the seat pads and found beneath it a label of the John Wanamaker Store in Philadelphia, proof that they had passed through that store's antique gallery. Further comparison with the Winterthur chair showed that even the faint marks of the clamps used in gluing the chairs matched.

The chairs were auctioned in late November 1975 and were bought by Israel Sack, the New York dealer, for $207,500—more than twenty times the top value placed on them in London.

To give some measure of how prices for fine American cabinetry have soared in recent years, in April 1961, in the sale of the Lewis Collection at Parke Bernet, the highest price reached in the dispersal of this fine collection was $26,000 paid for a slant-front desk. The set of hairy-paw foot chairs brought the highest price of any set of chairs at auction. In January 1977, Israel Sack, the New York dealer in American furniture, paid $135,000 for a Chippendale carved mahogany bombé chest made in the Boston area, circa 1765–80. He also paid $85,000 for a Queen Anne shell-carved walnut wing chair. The previous high for a piece of American furniture

*An American early nineteenth-century Sheraton mahog-
any swell-front bureau with fluted legs running its full
height, $350.*

was $120,000 paid for a Goddard-Townsend kneehole desk during
the 1972–73 season. The Lewis Collection slant-front desk is now
in the Henry Ford Museum in Dearborn, Michigan.

For those who are planning to buy antiques on a budget for use
in their homes, the foregoing is still of more than educational interest. The history of art and antiques buying is replete with stories
of unknown works by great artists and artisans turning up in unexpected places, bought for a fraction of their value. So it is useful to
know at least the names of the major American artisans and to
study some of the characteristics of their style and details of their
workmanship, all of which are available in more specialized books,
so that the awareness of their distinctive characteristics will always

be in the back of your mind as you do your browsing for pieces you can afford.

As we move inland from the port cities, the character of the furniture changes from quality cabinetry in fine woods such as walnut and mahogany, to early American country furniture made of cherry, maple, oak, pine or other fir (known collectively as deal), or other woods common to the forests of the American countryside in pioneer days. These pieces range from rough-hewn utility articles that we associate with huge kitchens—vast open fireplaces equipped with wrought-iron implements, deal tables, dough boxes, spinning wheels—to more finished ladder-back and rush-seat chairs, corner cabinets, chests, and bedsteads with posts and canopies, often well made and graceful in line, much in demand through all changes in taste, and abundantly available at every country auction as well as many city auctions.

If you live, for instance, in the Washington, D.C., area and are looking for Early American cabinetry or country furniture, consider some of the pieces you might have bought at the auction galleries of Adam A. Weschler & Son at a recent sale. The descriptions are often sparse—not surprising since the sales catalogues usually list 1,200–1,500 lots—but Weschler is one of the auction houses outside New York City that makes a real effort to provide reasonably accurate identifications.

In reading the descriptions and prices that follow, keep in mind some of the prices you have paid, or have been asked, for comparable contemporary pieces or modern copies of these antiques. Not all the items listed are within the modest budget we have been emphasizing. The more expensive pieces listed are mentioned as firm evidence that there are variances in quality, workmanship, and authenticity that justify higher prices for some items in today's market. Remember, too, that we are talking of prices at the recent peak for American antiques.

If you were furnishing a bedroom in American antiques, this is part of the choice you might have had: An American cherry and pine high-post bed with canopy, circa 1810, $320. With it you might have wanted an American Hepplewhite inlaid cherry four-drawer chest, circa 1810, with some original brasses, $425. As a jewelry box, your eye may have been caught by an antique miniature chest of drawers, circa 1760, 14 inches high, to stand on the chest, $150. Or perhaps you would prefer something with a mirror —an antique American Sheraton mahogany five-drawer shaving

A wide selection of fine Early American glass.

mirror with ivory ball feet, 28 inches high, $135. Or a Chippendale
mahogany mirror for the wall over the chest at $250. In the place
of the chest you might have chosen a Pennsylvania sponge-decor-
ated and painted three-drawer lift-top dower chest, circa 1810,
$225. Or a Rhode Island Hepplewhite mahogany dressing table,
circa 1800, with ebony ball and dart inlay on the front legs, $550,
which goes with a similarly inlaid three-drawer dressing mirror,
circa 1815, $200.

This is a Federal giltwood and gesso wall mirror,
circa 1810.

You might have preferred another bed, perhaps an antique four-poster with a mattress and spring, for only $90, which would leave more for other pieces in a modest budget. So would an American Chippendale pine lift-top dower chest, Pennsylvania, circa 1825, $85, less decorative, perhaps, than the painted chest, but much cheaper, too. Which might make possible a six-drawer Sheraton New York chest, circa 1820, with pineapple carved feet, $325. Or an American cherry and mahogany bow-front four-drawer chest, circa 1800, with a later American walnut shaving mirror with one drawer, $175. And to complete the furnishings, for $135, an antique American Belter-type carved rosewood slipper chair with a needlepoint seat.

As for decorations, the choice is almost unlimited. If you selected all the least expensive major pieces listed above and wanted to splurge on a bedcovering, you might choose, for $575, an old Chinese brocaded silk bride's bedcover in gold with an elaborate brocaded scene of flowers, butterflies, and birds, 86 by 108 inches. Or you might settle for two antique samplers, one dated 1799, the other 1827, for $130. Or a handwork antique jacquard cover signed "Catherine Knabb" and dated 1841, $170. Or seven pieces of antique Mary Gregory cranberry glass for $275. Or you might want a collection of fifty-five early eighteenth-century Dutch and French engravings, enough to decorate all your halls and spare bedrooms and to do groupings in your living room, from the Springfield (Massachusetts) Museum, for $225.

Every conceivable kind of early American workmanship is desirable and available. All of it lends itself well to any decor, from hand-hammered iron hinges and locks and old wagon wheels that inevitably end up as chandeliers to early glass and silver, which is of fine quality and can be costly if it is eighteenth century.

There are, perhaps, special reasons why these sales are so rich in the choices they offer and so inviting in the prices the objects bring. Washington is a city of transients. It has fewer antique shops, probably, than another city of its size. Its surrounding countryside is dotted with stately homes furnished a hundred years ago or more, whose contents come on the market in a steady flow as families die out, or the land around the homes is sold to developers. The sales are big—as many as 1,200 items at a time, spread over three or four days. The capacity of a city to absorb such a quantity of antiques and objects, where people tend to live in small housekeeping apartments or hotel rooms, is limited.

But apart from the fact that Washington is the nation's capital, it is no different from any other city with an old hinterland that is undergoing change. It is this that makes buying at auction for use so very attractive.

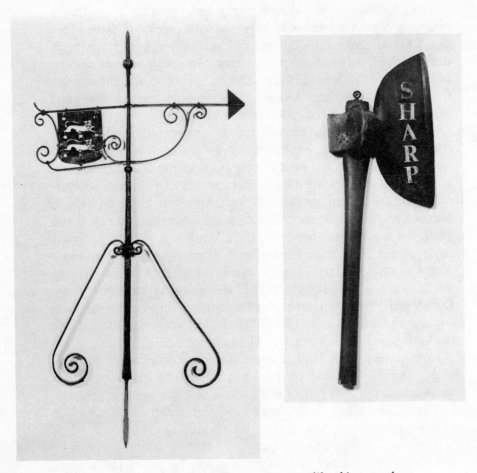

*Articles made for utilitarian purposes, like this ax-trade
sign and weathervane, now are used for interior decoration.*

Oriental art objects have a place in a chapter on Americana because there is a natural bridge between the two, called Chinese Export porcelain, made for the American taste—often to American
design—from the eighteenth century onward. It was frequently
made on order with a family crest or coat of arms as the central
decorative motif. A large dinner service of export porcelain bearing the emblem of The Society of the Cincinnati was made for
George Washington. Another, made for Martha Washington, has
her initials on each piece and the names of the thirteen states

This Pennsylvania nineteenth-century watercolor picture of a flower-filled vase brought $200 at auction.

around the borders. Pieces from these collections are in many museums and occasionally others come on the market from private collections. Pieces from such famous services, particularly the Cincinnati service, bring prices of $5,000 and more. The more ordinary pieces—those without strong historical associations—are plentiful and often at modest prices, even today.

Dinner services for later Presidents were often made by the great French porcelain factories at Limoges. A dish from such a service, made for President Lincoln by Haviland, recently sold for $4,500 at auction. Six dinner plates from a service made for President Harrison at Limoges recently sold for $5,900, a shade under an average $1,000 a plate.

So-called "Chinese Lowestoft" porcelain, sometimes confused with Chinese Export, emanated in fact from kilns in England with often poorly copied Chinese designs and is relatively unimportant. All through the nineteenth century and even later, China exported porcelain to the United States, not only in the form of services for American families but in copies of earlier pieces for the growing mercantile trade of this expanding country. The quantities were enormous and such pieces abound. They have no great value as antiques, but are of undeniable beauty, well worth having and exhibiting as objects of art. These pieces were made for the dining rooms of the wealthy middle classes. But there was another category of China, known under the all-inclusive name of Cantonware, although much of it came from other big port cities. It was brought back as ballast in the bottoms of ships whose main cargo was the delicate silks, teas, and spices of the Orient and served the purpose of protecting this precious cargo against water seepage in the bottoms of the holds. Cantonware, also called Willowware, is blue and white, the designs often including an arched footbridge over a stream with pagoda or the facade of a house, sometimes with figures, sometimes not, but always with a willow tree by the bridge. Pieces of this kind were made for the kitchen tables, were sturdy and consequently had a good rate of survival. They are now being avidly collected by those interested in Americana and prices are rising. A good-sized Canton platter today may bring $100 or more whereas a few years ago it might have sold for $15 or $20.

There is no limit to the variety of objects of Americana that are collected today, and the bicentennial of American Independence sharply increased prices for most of them. Even the simplest bit of metalwork—a hinge, a candleholder, a cast-iron doorstop, Indian basketry, and articles of clothing, not to mention rugs and pottery —is in demand. Silver from the hand of Paul Revere, his stamp unmistakable in the graceful lines he gave to bowls and teapots, still survives, and pieces are occasionally traded in the auction market for many thousands of dollars. A single Revere tablespoon recently sold for $425. But the lesser pieces of silver by American makers of the nineteenth century often sell for relatively modest sums. Recently two silver porringers, one from 1802, the other from 1826, were sold at Weschler's in Washington for $80 and $100. Curiously enough, a coffee service consisting of an urn, sugar bowl, and creamer, made by S. Kirk & Son, of Baltimore, which attested that the replacement value of the three pieces today would be in excess of $12,000, went as a lot for $4,000 in the same sale.

The first sale of Indian basketry at Sotheby Parke Bernet brought some astonishing prices—as much as $3,000 for a single example of great beauty. Then there came a flood of such collections, and prices have now subsided to the point where one can buy highly decorative Indian basketry for as little as $25.

Almost any kind of early American metalwork is now eagerly collected. Bell metal is preferred over brass for andirons, for instance, a pair selling for as high as $1,000, while the brass andirons that were characteristic of the early nineteenth century seldom bring more than $350 and often can be bought for as little as $100. On the other hand, a bell-metal ladle, with a maker's mark indicating it came from the forge of W. Barton in the early nineteenth century, recently sold for $275.

American glass is such a broad and varied category, with a range of prices that goes up into the tens of thousands, that it simply cannot be dealt with in this kind of book. There is so much of it and it is so attractive that a little study would be worthwhile for anyone interested in acquiring Americana for decorative purposes. You will find pieces in little shops for under $100, but at major auctions of Americana, the prices may well be beyond your reach.

American embroidery, stumpwork pictures, Pennsylvania Dutch *frakturs* (embroidered mottoes and pictures), patchwork quilts—all are such a craze at this point that you will have to just trust to luck to find something worth having at a price you can afford. Frakturs now sell sometimes for as much as $2,000! Early American wood pieces—treen, the English call them—are still a buy within reach and often are attractive with the patina that old wood takes on from handling. I think particularly of turned candlesticks and bowls of one kind or another. Carved wood of all kinds, from duck decoys to cigar store Indians, abound. The decoys sell for $25 and up and, if they have not been repainted or otherwise restored, are attractive pieces for a mantel or bookshelf. Carved wood toys of all kinds are now being collected, as are dolls, long a favorite of many. Cast-iron toy banks, early electric trains, early tools and weapons, from cavalry sabers of the Civil War to Colt weapons of the early twentieth century, are now rising rapidly in cost.

In short, there is almost no area of American life of the past that is not rich in things to be collected—things of beauty with style and line and the hand of ancestral workmen plainly evident, all of which are an asset to the decor of any American home.

CHAPTER

12

THE REVIVAL IN AMERICAN ART

FOR YEARS, while prices of European paintings were rising toward the stratosphere, American collectors pursued them until they were quite out of reach. Only then did they turn their eyes toward the long neglected area of American art. With few exceptions, collectors had ignored American painting, although there was a vigorous art tradition in this country dating from the earliest settlers and stemming from their European origins. Most serious collectors and museums tended to disdain paintings by Americans, unless, like Benjamin West, the eighteenth-century academician, or Mary Cassatt, the twentieth-century American Impressionist, they had studied and worked abroad and so had become part of the mainstream of European, rather than American, art.

West, painter of huge historical scenes and heroic portraits of majestic size, was born in Springfield, Pennsylvania, not far from Philadelphia, in 1738. He began his career as a simple painter of primitive portraits and Pennsylvania rural scenes. But at the time of his death in 1820, he was Historical Painter to King George III of England and president of the British Royal Academy, which he had helped to found. West made this unlikely and impressive transition by attracting the attention of influential patrons in Philadelphia, where he had established a thriving studio as a portrait painter at eighteen. They recognized his talent and sent him to Italy to study, and he never returned to the country of his birth.

What makes West important on the American scene is not only his own painting, but his influence on a long list of American artists who went to London to study with him and in later years with other members of the Royal Academy. Most notable were Gilbert Stuart, the most famous of Washington's portraitists; Charles Willson Peale and Rembrandt Peale, of the large Peale family of artists; Mathew Pratt; Samuel F. B. Morse, a portrait painter and founder of the National Academy of Design, who built on the theories of Ampère to perfect a system of telegraphy. Also Robert Fulton, a gunsmith, as well as landscape and portrait painter, who built the first successful American steamboat, the Clermont, popularly called Fulton's Folly; John Singleton Copley, Washington Allston, John Trumbull, and undoubtedly others who followed them to England and the European continent.

Most American painters of the Revolutionary and post-Revolutionary period began and ended their careers as primitive painters, either as amateurs who painted for the love of it, or artisans—sign painters who also did portraits of innkeepers, their ladies and their children, as well as for anyone else who could pay a modest fee.

Some became richly accomplished, learning by instincts the tricks of perspective that lifted them above the simple primitives who recorded what they saw in flat terms with a distorted view of distance, depth, and size. Understanding their work is what someone described as "the appreciation of the art of the un-selfconscious by the selfconscious."

The American primitive best known to us today is Grandma Moses, Anna Mary Robertson Moses, probably because hers was a more contemporary fame; she died in 1961 and her discovery touched off a revival of interest in other primitives. She faithfully recorded a country lifetime with complete naïveté which won her acclaim.

American primitive painting occupies a role in fine art comparable with the Italian primitives of the thirteenth and fourteenth centuries, with the primitive rendering of household scenes on Greek vases, with the primitive wall paintings in the caves of Southern France, or in the tombs of Egypt's pharaohs. All are the work of the un-selfconscious who have set down with the materials at hand what they could see, as it appeared to them to be most accurately rendered on a two-dimensional surface.

There are some great American collections of primitive art. One of the most important was that formed by Edgar William and Bernice Chrysler Garbisch, now in the National Gallery of Art in Washington. The Garbisch collection was begun in 1940, long before the revival of interest in American art, and constitutes nearly three thousand paintings. The earliest pictures in the collection

*This striking American primitive of a person named
Emma Van Name by an unknown artist illustrates all
the characteristics of primitive painting.*

"The Cat" by an unknown American primitive painter, circa 1840.

were painted around 1710, the latest toward the close of the nineteenth century.

The best way to understand primitive painting is to look at it. In
particular, the painting of Emma Van Name, by an unknown artist, circa 1795, which is reproduced herewith. Is Emma a child or a
grown woman? The face is ageless, the hands are babyish. The
clothes indicate the child, the proportions a woman. There is an at-
tempt at perspective, but it seems all wrong. Everything is out of
proportion, particularly the goblet from which she is eating berries,
whether she is a little girl or a grown woman. It is a naïve work by
a true primitive, the colors flat, the proportions distorted.

*"On Point" by D. G. Stouter, an American primitive
painter, circa 1840.*

Two famous woodland scenes, also from the Garbisch collection, show the problems of proportion and perspective even more dramatically. In both cases the artist may have wanted to show the cat and dog as huge, menacing creatures to the birds and the grouse. Not only is the result one of outlandish exaggeration, but· the cat seems lacking a body, a head partly buried in the grass. And the dog seems unstable in the space it occupies.

*An American primitive portrait of two children by an
unknown nineteenth-century artist.*

There is a list in the appendix of some known primitive artists
who worked in America from the early 1700s onward, giving the
dates when they were known to have flourished, if available, and
the region in which they lived and worked. It is there purely for
reference. Any American primitive painting you may find, and
they are plentiful in antique shops and at auction sales throughout
the Northeast states, is worth acquiring, again if it pleases your
taste and the price is not too high. Generally primitive portraits
sell for around $500.

Every piece and object in this apartment is Art Nouveau, bought before the present enthusiasm for the period sent prices sky high. Not everyone would want to live with a single period so sharply delineated as this room is. But it does have a very definite impact.

WILLIAM DOUGLAS KING

This is a turn-of-the-century bedroom in a house furnished otherwise in early American pieces. Apart from the coverlet and draperies, everything is old, if not really "antique." The brass bed makes the room a smashing success.

The Ming Dynasty pottery horse goes well with pages of Persian calligraphy framed in a hand illuminated mat in gold of the period—the eighteenth century—and giltwood monstrance from a medieval church balancing the oriental sage at right.

The Italian walnut chest is late sixteenth or early seventeenth century with original hardware. Its top is battered and nicked, but nevertheless it is a handsome piece in this Greenwich Village foyer in New York City. The painting of Moses above it is an "Old Master" that emerged from years of grime and coats of old varnish in a process of cleaning that cost more than the picture.

A still life with apples by Silas Martin, painted in 1889.

You will find that primitives run heavily to portraits of husbands and wives and children. The little girls often are dressed in the long white gowns of Emma's period, in dresses with lacy pants showing beneath the hems. Boys wear dark suits or tight white trousers like those of the fathers—little men, except for their childish faces.

One also finds country scenes and marine paintings, particularly in New England, where paintings of ships were often commissioned by their proud owners. At auction good marine paintings will sometimes sell as high as $10,000, but they can often be bought for under $500 at country sales.

It is interesting to note that the Garbisches hung fine Impressionist and Post-Impressionist paintings in their home in New York City, but the walls of their Maryland manor house were hung with American primitives in settings of Early American furnishings.

You cannot go wrong by following their example.

Primitive painters represent only a small segment of American art. By far the largest group was sophisticated painters who bor-

A 1904 painting by Walter Gay called "Reveillon Interior,"
18 by 21½ inches, sold at auction for $400.

rowed from their European contemporaries. In the eighteenth century, English portraiture was the dominant influence, starting with Benjamin West and John Singleton Copley, and continuing through the decades to the highly experimental work being done by artists today.

Perhaps the most fascinating group of artists in our history were the members of the Peale family of Philadelphia. Charles Willson Peale (1741–1827) believed that anyone could be taught to paint. He tested this belief by teaching his brother James what he had learned about painting during his studies in England. He named his sons after famous artists. There were Rembrandt Peale, Raphaelle

A bronze by Bessie Potter Vonnoh, 17½ inches high, $800.

Peale, Titian Peale, and Rubens Peale. All became painters, as did his daughters, Maria, Anna Claypoole, and Margaretta Angelica Peale. All lived well into the second half of the nineteenth century and were prolific and talented artists.

Rembrandt Peale is perhaps the best known, for he painted portraits of George Washington, many of which have been copied

*A bronze bas-relief, "Portrait of Virginia Gerson,"
by William O'Donovan (1844–1920), $350.*

and recopied by lesser artists, some of whom even faithfully copied his signature. Rubens Peale and his sisters were dedicated mainly to still lifes of fruits and flowers. The others were portrait painters and landscape artists, and paintings by all of them keep turning up in unexpected corners.

In the nineteenth century, after the invention of the camera, interest in portrait painting slackened as photographers began providing the family likenesses that were so important at the time as, indeed, they are today. Photography of the nineteenth century has now become an important area for collecting, as has photographic equipment which is sold regularly at auction. At the same time, photography is now taking its rightful place as an art form

Charles Dana Gibson, a popular illustrator in the early years of the century, has come into prominence as an artist whose drawings are much sought after. This one brought $500 at auction.

through the efforts of such historians as Peter Pollack, author of the *Picture History of Photography*, and others. Photography is exhibited regularly in such prestigious settings as the Museum of Modern Art in New York. New York now has a museum called The Center for Photography.

In the nineteenth century, artists turned more and more to landscapes and to paintings depicting the life of the times, particularly in the then still wild and woolly West. Many artists went on expeditions of exploration and faithfully recorded in watercolor life among the Indians on the Western Plains. Alfred Jacob Miller was one of the most prolific of this group. Western landscapes by such artists as Thomas Moran and Albert Bierstadt are now in great demand, as are pictures by members of the Hudson River school, such as Jasper Francis Cropsey.

A theorem painting inscribed: "Sacred to the memory of Whitney Scovill and Whitney Tyler Scovill," by an anonymous New England artist, dated 1840, painted in black on white velvet, showing a woman in mourning costume weeping before a tombstone, $175 at auction.

Watercolor was a favorite medium of nineteenth-century American artists, although they also worked extensively in oil. The technique of applying color soluble in water is a difficult one, and American watercolor technique is in some instances superior to that of the leading English watercolorists. Certainly no one need ever apologize for hanging a good nineteenth-century watercolor by an American artist.

So much has happened in American painting since the dawn of the twentieth century that it would take another book to en-

A pair of watercolors by N. Moore.

compass it all. Works by artists of the period preceding World War II will probably be prohibitively high, because they are much in demand, even drawings and prints. But bargains do come on the market, usually out of ignorance on the part of the seller. So as a buyer, you must be prepared to take full advantage of such ignorance whenever and wherever you encounter it.

What is in this book is not enough to give you the advantage you must have if you are to buy worthwhile pictures at a price you can afford. All we have tried to do in these pages is to make you less self-conscious about fine art, to give you the courage to reject the junk out of hand, as well as the courage to buy a picture simply because it appeals to you, even though the name of the artist may not set bells ringing and lights flashing in your head.

CHAPTER

13

PRINTS, THE SPRINGBOARD TO COLLECTING

THERE ARE still other important areas to explore.

One is the world of prints.

Their appeal is tremendous for the person of limited resources who is looking for fine art to decorate his walls. They offer broad and inviting possibilities as a relatively inexpensive way to add areas of color to the walls of a home. Many a collector took the first tentative exploratory steps toward assembling what has later become a distinguished collection by buying a single print.

But many a beginner has become discouraged, has felt himself victimized by buying what he thought was an original print, only to learn that it was a cheap reproduction. The purpose of this chapter is to arm the reader, as far as possible, against this danger, with the caveat that must be emphasized here that even experts can be fooled by some reproductions.

In the context of our view on buying art and antiques, there is nothing wrong, however, with a good reproduction. What is wrong is to pay original print prices for something that is worth only a few dollars. The opportunities to make this mistake are endless and the pitfalls are deep and hard to get around. But there are a few sound guideposts. To follow them it is useful to read a primer on the subject. A good one is the pamphlet edited by Joshua Binion Cahn for the Print Council of America.*

Prints are multiples, to use a popular current term for works produced in series from an original design which includes, also, casts of sculpture. The fact that they are produced in series, in an edition, opens the way for myriad complications.

Often prints are produced by what must be considered, in the broadest sense, mechanical means. That is, in some kind of press.

* *What Is an Original Print?* Print Council of America, 572 Madison Avenue, New York, N.Y. 10022. 1961.

The hand of the artist—the one ingredient that is essental in the creation of a true work of art—can be evidenced only to a degree, which varies with the technique employed. The extent to which the artist participates in the final act of creating the finished product is one of the factors that modifies the validity of the print as an original work of art. To put that another way, in the making of a print, the hand of the artist is likely to be more or less remote from the finished print. The degree of remoteness is one of the factors to be considered in deciding whether a print is an original.

Some printmaking techniques—lithography, for one—usually require the services of a technician to do the actual printing. The prints produced by such techniques, under the control or supervision of the artist, are original works of art.

There are four basic techniques for making prints:

Woodcuts and other relief processes. In these processes, part of the flat surface of a block is cut away leaving only the desired printing image raised. The raised printing image is then inked and brought into contact under pressure with the paper or other material on which the print is to be made. This may be done in a press, or by hand, using a hand roller. Material for blocks that are used in making such prints includes, in addition to wood, linoleum (much favored by Picasso and a technique that has produced some of his finest prints), cardboard, lucite, chipboard, various types of composition board, plaster board, and cut paper. For prints made on cardboard or paper surfaces, the printing image is built up in layers, instead of being cut away.

Etchings and other intaglio processes. These are the opposite of the relief processes in that the image to be printed is cut into the plate or other surface and the ink is laid onto the paper from the resulting grooves or indentations. Acid is used in the case of metal plates, to etch out the design, in addition to special hand tools with which the artist literally draws on the metal by cutting into it. Such plates are generally of copper, but other metals such as zinc or aluminum are also used. Intaglio plates can also be cut into plastics such as lucite. Engravings, etchings, aquatints, mezzotints, and drypoints are all made by the intaglio press, each using a variation on the basic technique. More than one technique can be used on a single print (as well as a mixture of other processes) in which case the technique may be called "mixed media."

Lithography, which is based on the natural tendency of an oily surface to reject water, is the process that has been the most highly

*A collection of prints can be started with very little money. Once
begun, such a collection can be improved by selling pieces that
have gained in value to buy more important works. As an example,
this etching is from the 1822 edition of the Works of William
Hogarth, which consisted of 119 plates. The entire set sold at auction for $325. Less than $4.00 each!*

refined in its mechanical development—and the most abused. In
lithography the image is made on a stone or on a zinc plate with a
grease-based substance—crayon, if the image is drawn on the plate
by hand, or photographically, using a chemical which leaves a deposit of grease if it is done mechanically. Water adheres to the surface of the plate but not to the oily design. An oil-based ink is used
which is rejected by the film of water on the plate and adheres
only to the oily design, from which it is transferred to the printing
surface.

Silk screen and other stencil processes involve applying ink to
exposed or cut-out portions of the pattern so it comes through
onto the printing surface. Serigraphy is the modern name for silk-
screen printing, a method that is growing rapidly in importance

Thomas Hart Benton's farm scene, entitled "Rainy Day," one of an edition of 250 lithographs, signed by the artist, dated 1938, which sold at auction for $300.

today. The silk or similar material is stretched on a frame and its threads are sealed with a lacquer or similar substance except for the design that is to be printed. Ink is then forced through the exposed areas of the material to the paper, using a roller, resulting in a textured finish that other processes do not provide. Serigraphy is often combined with one of the intaglio processes in producing finished prints, the etching or engraving laying down the design and the silk screen providing the color.

Any of these techniques may be used to produce an original print. In some cases the artist may be sufficiently expert in the techniques and materials used to produce the final print himself. Usually the artist calls upon a technician to transfer his original design to paper. The great Japanese wood-block prints of the seventeenth and eighteenth centuries were generally made from

"Study of My Mother" by George Bellows, a 1921 lithograph by the American artist, signed and titled in pencil and framed, $450.

blocks cut by a professional woodcutter—the equivalent of the engraver or lithographer today—not by the artist.

Today many artists are reverting to the concept of the artist as printmaker. In many parts of the country artists have formed print centers where they have revived the old techniques, acquired the necessary equipment and materials, and are not only producing prints of their own works by traditional methods, but are developing new techniques and materials for this purpose. Prints actually

MARTIN GORDON GALLERY, INC.

*A Whistler etching of the section of London harbor called Bil-
lingsgate, dated 1859. Framed, it sold for $250.*

produced by the artists themselves are, of course, the purest of the
pure.

Numbers are important to the collector of prints who is concerned with the aesthetic purity of the work of art, as well as with
its rarity. As the number of prints in an edition increases, their
value to the collector as works of art also diminishes.

It is reasonable to assume that a lithograph or a serigraph can be
reproduced indefinitely, with no apparent difference to the eye in
the quality of the print, until the stone, or plate, or stencil begins
to deteriorate and show signs of wear. Yet an early impression is
likely to be more highly valued by a collector than an identical
later impression. It is for this reason that numbered prints are numbered in sequence—3/10, meaning the third impression pulled in an

A 1916 etching and drypoint by Childe Hassam, American Impressionist whose paintings sell for upward of $35,000. Titled "Newport Harbor," this print sold for $225.

edition of ten, rather than merely "one of an edition of ten." This is true, also, of casts of sculpture.

These are truths that any collector would accept as indisputable, but they are true only in a relative sense. To explain what we mean by that, let us look at some examples.

A recent sale of prints at the auction gallery of Kornfeld & Klipstein in Berne, Switzerland, caused a sensation in art circles be-

A fine André Masson lithograph of a nude torso,
$1,900 at auction.

cause of the high prices reached. One part of the sale consisted of prints by Picasso from the collection formed by Georges Bloch, author of a definitive catalogue of Picasso's graphic works.

The most important print in that collection was an impression of "The Frugal Repast," a black-and-white etching made in 1904 in Paris. There were thirty impressions, signed and some with inscriptions by the artist dedicating them to individuals to whom he gave the prints, in that original edition. The example from the Bloch collection brought $162,750, to which must be added the Swiss tax on such purchases at auction of 10 per cent, bringing the total price to $180,000.

In 1913, the French publisher Ambroise Vollard bought the zinc plate. He had it faced with steel, a delicate process which preserves the original plate to reduce wear. From the steel-faced plate, two editions were published. The first consisted of twenty-seven or

Reginald Marsh's famous 1936 etching of Coney Island Beach, one of five proofs from the early state, signed in pencil by Marsh's wife. It sold for under $500.

twenty-nine prints (the exact number is not known) which became Print No. 1 in a portfolio of Picasso etchings called *"Les Saltimbanques."* Examples of "The Frugal Repast" from that edition have a value on the New York print market of $60,000 to $75,000, depending upon the condition.

The third and last edition of the print taken from the original plate after it was steel-faced consisted of two hundred fifty impressions which are valued in New York today at $25,000 to $35,000.

If all the prints taken from the original plate before and after it was steel-faced were to change hands at the prices prevailing in that sale, their total value would be in excess of $12 million.

In the same sale there was another rare and much-sought-after print called "Minotauromachie," of which only five impressions are known to exist. There were no editions other than the original edition printed in Paris. The whereabouts of the plate are not known. Yet this print was valued in the Bloch sale at less than the print of "The Frugal Repast." It was bought for \$126,700 by a Swiss collector.

It is reasonable to assume that if there had been only five prints made of "The Frugal Repast," its value would have been even greater. And if there had been three editions of the "Minotauromachie," instead of one of five known impressions, its value would be lower.

In spite of the fact that there are so many more prints of "The Frugal Repast" in circulation or in collections all over the world, it is valued higher than the much rarer "Minotauromachie," because it appeals more to the eye—its aesthetic value is greater.

Consider another example, from an earlier sale of Picasso prints by the same auction house. One was *"Tête de Femme IV,"* an aquatint, one of an edition of six produced in 1935. It was an artist's proof, signed at lower right and inscribed by the artist *"Bon à tirer,"* which means that Picasso approved that print as a proof for the edition before the other impressions were taken. The print brought \$51,000. It is reasonably safe to assume that if there had been only three impressions in that edition, the price might have been somewhat higher.

Another fine head of a woman in the same sale, *"La Femme aux Cheveux Verts,"* was a colored lithograph produced in 1949 in an edition of fifty examples, each signed and numbered. It brought \$15,000. It is reasonable to assume that its market value would have been higher if the edition had been smaller. Would it have been worth \$51,000 if only six impressions were known to have been pulled? That would depend upon the aesthetic judgment of the bidders comparing the two prints. It might have been worth more. It also might have been worth less.

If Picasso himself had pulled each of twenty-five prints from the stone, wood block or lino, had himself discarded those that were not quite right, and had signed those of which he approved, they would have a greater value than if he had turned over his design to a lithographer and had merely supervised his work, approving a final proof with his signature before leaving the printing to the technicians.

If Picasso had merely dropped off his design at the lithographer's shop, with his notes as to color, then had gone off to raise money for the Spanish Republicans, the resulting prints would have less value.

One of Magritte's favorite themes, the man in the bowler hat with a green apple hiding his face, has become a widely circulated poster.

The numbering of a print tells us how many prints were authorized by the artist in the edition. But it is no guarantee that more
were not printed. The lithographer may have run off an additional
five or fifty prints for himself, either with or without the permis-
sion of the artist, and without numbering them. These prints
would be unsigned. They would be less valuable than the numbered prints in the authorized original edition. The artist, too, may
have produced prints for his own uses, outside the regular edition.
These may be called "Artist's Proofs," or, in France, "*hors com-
merce*" prints, meaning not to be sold, or, "*Épreuve de l'artiste.*"

After the death of René Magritte, the Belgian surrealist, his
widow arranged for the printing of relatively large editions of lithographs for which the artist had completed the original designs.
They were small prints and were issued in numbered editions of
two hundred fifty, signed in imitation of the artist's hand by his
widow. They have a value on today's market of several hundred
dollars, whereas original prints produced by Magritte during his
lifetime, signed and numbered by him, might be worth several
thousand dollars. Yet, aesthetically speaking, are the posthumous
prints less desirable than those dating from the artist's lifetime? To
a collector they are. But a noncollector might well consider such a
print a bargain at $500. And who is to say he is wrong?

There is another clinker in all of this. Modern technology has
made it possible to produce generation after generation of editions
of prints that often can hardly be told from examples in the original edition. Sometimes they are bootlegged, even while the artist is
still alive.

Prints in large editions can be produced in modern offset presses
by photographing an original print, using the same color separa-
tion process that produces the superb reproductions we see in contemporary art books. Copies can be made in an almost unlimited
number from metal plates.

At this point a print ceases to have aesthetic value as a work of
art and its market value can be no more than a few dollars. It is a
printed reproduction of a work of art, no different from, say, a
printed reproduction of the "Mona Lisa." Such a reproduction is
worth no more than the cost of the paper, ink, press-time, and labor
that went into producing it.

There have been many attempts to establish guidelines for print
buyers and to draft definitions to protect the public, but their
value is highly questionable. A rule or definition that is fully appli-

cable to one period in the history of printmaking is meaningless in another.

Mark E. Rosen, head of the Print Department at Sotheby Parke Bernet, has a simple—and convincing—definition for a contemporary print.

"An original print today," he says, "is anything the artist says it is." This means that if an artist designs a print, gives it to a technician to print as a serigraph, and accepts the result as an original print, then none can dispute this. This seems logical. It has long been accepted that the artist is the best judge of his own work. During his lifetime Picasso received a constant flow of photographs of works attributed to him, often bearing his signature. If they were indeed his, he would scrawl on the back the word *"vrai,"* which means true. If not, he would scribble the word *"fausse"* (false) across the face of the photograph, often with the brush and pigment he happened to be using at the moment.

The world of the collector being what it is, if Picasso went so far as to scrawl his signature beneath his verdict, even a photograph of a fake Picasso took on a certain value as an autograph.

The Rosen definition would tend to end the controversy that has swirled around some prints by famous artists who have been criticized for authorizing editions of prints to which their only contribution was the original design. Some critics of contemporary printmaking policy still adhere to the old purist definition which holds that

> To qualify as an original print, the artist must have made the image on the plate, stone, wood block, or other material that is used in creating the finished work.

The trouble with such a definition is that it would rule out many prints that have been collected since the birth of art—old master prints. What old master print would fit that definition, in the days when prints were made as reproductions of drawings and paintings? It was the *message* that was important, not the medium or the artist. "The Massacre of the Innocents," engraved by Marcantonio Raimondi in the sixteenth century, was cherished because of the picture it conveyed, not because it was from a drawing by Raphael.

It was the general practice in the early days of printmaking for the print to carry the name of the printmaker, as well as that of the artist. The engraving "Village Dance," for instance, has engraved

Le Message Biblique
de Marc Chagall

Musée du Louvre   Galerie Mollien

22 juin 2 octobre 1967 ouvert tous les jours sauf le mardi de 10 heures à 17 heures

Posters bought when they first come on the market can be acquired for a few dollars. Invariably, if they are by well-known artists, they rise in value over the years.

on the left "Rubens pinx," for "Rubens painted it," and on the right, "Bolswert sculpt," for "Bolswert engraved it."

Let us look at the lithograph by Chagall, made from the predominantly rust-red mural he painted for the Metropolitan Opera House at Lincoln Center, which was used as a poster heralding the opening of the new opera house. Chagall provided the basic art work for Mourlot, the Paris lithographer. Zinc lithographic plates were made from Chagall's design by Charles Sorlier, a master engraver. Chagall specified the colors and approved a final proof before the lithographs were printed. There was a limited edition of a hundred fifty, numbered and signed by Chagall. Then there were five thousand printed as posters, with the legend, "Metropolitan Opera House, Lincoln Center," at the top, printed over the design, and "Opening September 1966" at the bottom. The legend changed the work from a print to a poster. Printed in black in small letters at lower left is another legend: "D'après Marc Chagall —Ch. Sorlier, Grav." which means "after an original by Chagall, engraved by Charles Sorlier" and opposite that in white letters, "Printed in France—by Mourlot Paris."

The descriptive legend at the bottom of the Chagall poster, identifying and describing the role of those who had a hand in producing the prints, is essential in any case where someone other than the artist has a role of comparable importance in the making of a print. Those posters are considered original lithographic posters because Chagall supervised the final steps before the first print was produced and approved the plates and color. They were sold for $25 each. The signed version, before the addition of the legend, were sold for $200, most of the proceeds of both going to the Metropolitan Opera Company. Today, the posters that came out at $25 are being sold in poster shops for $200, and the signed and numbered version is bringing as much as $1,000.

How can one know, without devoting a lifetime to study, what is a good print? One doesn't, of course, and here again the question comes up as to whether we are buying as collectors or as home decorators. Even as home decorators, we are trying to buy things that are worth at least what we pay for them, which will retain their value and perhaps even increase in value over the years. There are ways that this can be done with minimal risk.

First, avoid buying framed prints at an auction, unless it is in an auction house that catalogues with care and stands behind what it says. If you see something at an exhibition that really sends you, ask if you can take the print from its frame to examine it. If this is permitted, there is a good chance that you will find a printer's name at the bottom, where it was hidden by the frame or mat. In that case it is an ordinary printed reproduction that was sold for as little as $1.00 when it was new. If you still want it, try to estimate the value of the frame and set a limit on what you will pay for it, commensurate with its nonvalue as a work of art.

Avoid buying prints at frame shops, or in artist supply shops, or, in fact, anywhere but from a reputable dealer who specializes in prints and will show them to you in a folio from which you can make a choice from among many. Start out by avoiding the popular names—Chagall, Picasso, Miro, Toulouse-Lautrec, Klee, etc. If you are unschooled in art, the chances are that prints by most artists whose names you will readily recognize as important will probably be beyond your pocketbook. Tell the dealer you want to look at prints within a price range that goes just below and just above the limit you have set for yourself. You will find prints in the $75 to $125 range, for instance, that will bear unfamiliar names, but many will please you. Select perhaps half a dozen prints you like well enough to want to hang on your walls and ask the dealer about the artists and about the type of print you have chosen by each. He will be glad to begin your education as to the technique used, the size of the edition, and something about the artist. Keep in mind that if you decide on a print by an artist you have never heard of, you will already be one up on anyone who admires it on your walls, because you will know what kind of print it is, when it was made, and something about the artist who designed it.

Even at major auction houses there will be many opportunities to buy prints in the price range you can afford. One of the major German houses regularly publishes print-sale catalogues in which are included only prints that are estimated to bring no more than 250 marks—about $125 at current rates of exchange. And these are original prints by artists of established reputations, although they may be unknown to you. Sotheby Parke Bernet still advertises that a substantial portion of the lots it sells are priced under $300. Many such lots are inexpensive prints.

When we talk of framed prints that sold originally for as little as a dollar, we are off in another realm where the entire reproduction process is mechanical, where not one, but several, technicians are called upon to contribute at various stages to the printing process, remote from the artist, often with no contact with him at all.

A Toulouse-Lautrec, created as a large billboard, 49½ by 35¼ inches, $3,000 at auction.

This is the world of reproductions.

They are produced in the same manner, essentially, as the fine reproductions we have come to expect in an expensive art book. A camera photographs an original, or even another good reproduction. The colors are separated by filters. Separate plates are exposed for each color and etched in an acid bath. In a shop concerned with turning out fine reproductions, there may be a certain amount of dot etching, in which an engraver working from a proof, lifts dots with great skill from portions of each plate where the color balance is off. The printing is in a high-speed press, either by direct transfer of the ink from the plate to the paper, or by the offset process in which the ink is transferred first to a rubber roller, called a blanket, which then lays the ink on the paper.

The result may be quite beautiful, as a color reproduction in an art book can be beautiful. But it is not a work of art, if only because the hand of the artist has not been involved, and it is a shame to pay fine art prices for such a product.

All of this would be devastatingly discouraging except for the one important fact that good, authentic prints can still be bought at relatively modest prices. It is not necessary to buy cheap reproductions. But there is nothing wrong with buying them, provided you know they are reproductions and you are paying for them as reproductions and not at the level of good prints.

Original posters are probably the least expensive of all prints. Produced by often well-known artists by lithography, silk screen, linoleum or wood-block cut, they can be bought for as little as $10. They will never be worth the prices that an original limited edition print brings. But they will always be worth what you paid for them, and may eventually increase in value, as has been the case with the Chagall Metropolitan Opera poster.

One striking indication of how a modest collection can grow in value is the experience of Peter Stone, the Broadway musical writer. Stone is a young man and he began buying posters perhaps fifteen years ago. Recently he gave his collection of 1,400 original posters to the Museum of Modern Art in New York. They were valued at $98,000. Most of them were bought for $5 or $10 at the time they were published. Some were signed by the artist and consequently cost more. But all together, they cost no more than a fraction of their value today.

CHAPTER

14

"THINGS"—THE LITTLE TREASURES

IN THE YEARS before World War I, the treasures that stirred the acquisitive instincts of the world's great collectors on both sides of the Atlantic were not old master paintings, nor yet the fine Post-Impressionist works then being created, but objects, dating from the eighteenth century back to antiquity. Delicate porcelain figures of shepherdesses from Dresden, rough stone sculptures from the Romanesque and Gothic periods, little Italian bronzes by Riccio and Giovanni of Bologna, majolica in all its varieties, T'ang horses, Chinese jades, Han bronzes, things of crystal, silver, gold snuffboxes, furniture delicately inlaid with marquetry and Sèvres porcelain plaques—sculptures of all sizes and categories and pictures, too, but drawings more importantly, and great prints. The museums that flourished in those days, most especially the Metropolitan Museum of Art in New York, mirror in their nonpainting collections the rich and varied tastes of those early twentieth-century collectors.

The vitrine, a glass-topped table with a velvet-lined compartment for displaying precious and perishable objects, was often the focus in fashionable salons, rather than what hung on the walls—unless they were decked with Beauvais or Gobelins tapestries. Today the vitrine has virtually disappeared from our homes. We see them most usually in little antique shops, used for small things that might otherwise go astray.

Many of those things—champlevé enamels from the twelfth century, Renaissance jewelry, carved ivory from the fourteenth century—are only now coming back to the price levels of the early 1900s and mainly because of a new generation of connoisseurs in Europe and not yet in the United States. It is significant that when the collection of Richard Weininger of New York was dispersed

*Since the Central American governments closed down on ex-
ports of pre-Columbian artifacts, prices in that region have
gone sky-high. Yet this handsome Costa Rican pottery head of
a man, the face red, the head buff, sold for only $650. The piece
opposite, shown full face, is a jar in the form of a head.*

in December 1972, it went to Christie's in London for sale, where
a superb marble bust of a young woman by Tullio Lombardi was
sold for $47,880, probably less than the collector paid for it when
he bought it in 1926 from Jacques Seligmann, the Paris art dealer.
A little bronze figure from the same collection, of a satyr by
Andrea Briosco, better known as Riccio, brought $85,680.*

In this country collecting of objects is mainly on three levels. At
the bottom is the magpie level—the accumulation of bits and pieces
of metal and glass and decorative objects; mementos, souvenirs,
things like barbed wire, for heaven's sake, examples of which are
avidly collected and even studied from books devoted to the subject; commemorative porcelains; cheap glassware from the depression period; bottles—the list would be almost endless.

At the top we collect stamps and coins, with a high level of appreciation and expertise in a booming market; eighteenth-century

* See International ART MARKET, Vol. XII, No. 12, pp. 266–67.

porcelains, English silver, orientalia—mainly Chinese porcelains and bronzes—and occasionally antiquities, an area most favored in this country by collectors of pre-Columbian artifacts and African art, for which there is also a big and flourishing market abroad. But an American collector might well hesitate to pay $47,880 for a superb sculpture by Tullio, or $85,000 for a rare and magnificent bronze by Riccio, when he could buy a misty Monet sketch of Waterloo Bridge, seen from the window of his room at the Savoy Hotel looking across the Thames for $67,200. After all, it would be chic to own a Monet—and who ever heard of Tullio Lombardi?

We also collect porcelain birds by Dorothy Doughty and Arnold Boehm, often paying more for those twentieth-century examples of porcelain sculpture than we do for lovely eighteenth-century birds decorated by Kaendler from the Meissen kilns in Dresden.

But generally we collect, in the middle level, objects for decorative purposes. A piece of porcelain, or silver, or glass to go just here, or just there in the decor of a living room or dining room, our main focus still being the pictures we hang on our walls.

We buy decorative objects of beauty when we can find them at
a price we can afford, whether old or new. We also look for exotic
things that will stir the curiosity—"conversation pieces" they are
called today—and in these there is great diversity to satisfy every
taste and pocketbook.

On a walk along Madison Avenue in the heart of New York's
art galleries and antique shops, I noted that the Graham Gallery,
near Seventy-ninth Street, was showing in its windows examples of
nineteenth-century scientific instruments and models of machinery.
Just down the street was a shop specializing in mineral specimens,
sea shells, and fossils—all highly decorative and calculated to excite
curiosity. My young daughter, always reluctant to express her
desires when asked what she wants for Christmas, when pressed
had asked for "a plain, round, purple whatever." I found one there
—a dried round, purple shell of a sea urchin from the English chan-
nel for $7.50.

Beyond this was another shop that specialized in old optical instruments and across the way, a shop dealing in military objects—
weapons, uniforms, field equipment such as brass canteens. On
down the avenue is another whose windows are periodically filled
with glass paperweights like a garden blooming under drab winter
skies.

The Graham Gallery, one of the oldest on Madison Avenue,
deals mainly in fine art—a wide variety of paintings, sculpture,
drawings, and prints, with emphasis on American art. But the
others are specialized shops, dealing in the objects that are suited to
today's life-style and today's pocketbooks, articles that fall under
the general heading of what I have called in these pages "things,"
because that is how I prefer to think of them. Whenever in the
past I have been involved in furnishing a home for myself, a substantial portion of my time and effort went into the accumulation
of things to put on the mantels or tables, to hang on doors, or to
dress up empty shelves, or simply to relieve the monotony of row
upon row of book bindings, decorative though these may be. To
give some perspective to the wide range that can be encompassed
by decorative objects of art, let us look at the dust jacket of a volume of *Art at Auction,* a book edited by Philip Wilson for
Sotheby & Company. It shows (Minerals indicated by dagger[†]):

1. A polished variscite† nodule from Utah.

2. A Kashmir green schist† figure of Vishnu, circa ninth century A.D.

These are all examples of American glass, mainly from the
eighteenth and nineteenth centuries. But any assortment of
glass, regardless of source or period, would enhance a dining
or living room if shown in this manner.

3. A Francesco Guardi Venetian landscape.
4. A Persian manuscript from a collection of poetry in a
   painted lacquer binding depicting the battle between the
   Moghul Army and Nadir Shah, nineteenth century.
5. A miniature of General Stevenson by John Smart, English
   miniaturist.
6. Two silver-gilt wine labels by Paul Storr, 1815.

7. Hanger Hill, etched by Graham Sutherland.

8. A gold nugget from California.

9. A Henry VII Apostle spoon, maker's mark a Gothic L, 1490.

10. A polished specimen of malachite† and azurite† combined, from Arizona.

11. A Louis XV gold and mother of pearl snuffbox by Jean Gaillard, Paris, 1745.

12. Two Japanese Kakiemon mandarin ducks, late seventeenth century.

13. A pre-Dynastic Egyptian slate pendant in the form of a bird.

14. A Persian miniature of a youth wearing a European hat, by Riza-i-Abbasi, circa 1630.

15. A North German or Lower Saxony bronze crucifix figure, twelfth century.

16. A Fabergé silver-gilt and enamel clock.

17. A nine-keyed boxwood clarinet by John Parker, London, circa 1800.

18. A Russian minature silver helmet of a Garde Cuirassier, late nineteenth century.

19. An amethyst† from Mexico.

20. Calcite† from Cumberland, England.

21. A Lorenzoni-type flintlock repeating pistol by Barber of London, circa 1760.

22. An Egyptian green-glazed composition Ushtabi figure.

23. Vanadinite† from Arizona.

24. A Ming blue and yellow dish, four-character mark of the Cheng Te reign, 1506–21.

That is only a brief part of the story. To list the wide range of items that come under the heading of objects of art could well take up a whole chapter, if not an entire book. So, let us try instead to arrive at a definition that covers such objects.

> An object of art is anything that displays artistry
> or artisanship in its conception and execution
> by the mind and the hand of man.

That sounds pretty good. But is it true? Does it go far enough? What about all those mineral specimens in that list and the shop dealing with fossils and sea shells in the heart of the art world on

Antiquities are still very much within reach and are a good buy. This Neo-Attic marble relief fragment, circa first century B.C., *of Hermes, his hair bound in a fillet, sold for $550.*

ALBERT AZZARRELLO.

The double-cyma curve of an American scythe handle contrasted with the cabriole leg of a Queen Anne nineteenth-century English chair. The chair languished in the author's barn for eight years, all four legs broken off by a workman who tilted it against a wall. Restored, it is a sturdy and handsome piece.

Madison Avenue in New York City? What about flowers and plants, fresh or dried, which are almost as important as man-made objects in focusing the eye and decorating a room?

Let's try again.

Anything that excites the eye or stimulates the visual imagination is an object of art.

There! That's better. But if that is true, it can be stated even more simply.

An object of art is anything you say it is.

That does it. "An object of art is anything you say it is." Quote and end quote. That says it all. That covers everything from the exquisite Bertoia fountains outside the Burlington Mills building on New York's Avenue of the Americas, which make the fine spray of water a part of the sculpture, to their counterpart in nature, the lavender thistle balls that grow wild by the pond outside my door; from the shards of pottery turned up by the plow of Mexican farmers to the bronze valve balanced on its stem in a block of ebony on the desk of a collector friend.

It covers, too, the handle of a scythe, exquisitely shaped in a perfect cyma curve, in delicate contrast with the tapering line of its gleaming blade. Most people know the scythe, or grass snath, only in crude representations in the hands of Father Time in newspaper cartoons marking the end of the old year. It is, in fact, a thing of beauty shaped in a graceful double curve of the finest ash, flowing in a smooth line from concave to convex, from its slender tip to the thicker steelbound base where the long cutting blade is attached.

The graceful lines of a scythe handle are dictated by its purpose, beauty added to utility, with two short handles set each at the apex of one of the double curves so the shaft of the handle passes smoothly by the body and the blade extends safely outward to cut long grasses or grains without maiming the user. It was in a restaurant on the shores of Schroon Lake in the Adirondacks, whose decor was otherwise as undistinguished as its cuisine, that I first saw a scythe handle on a wall decorated with obsolete farm and kitchen equipment. The scythe handle's relevance to the cabriole leg and back of a Queen Anne chair struck me forcibly. When I returned home I looked up what William Hogarth, the English painter and engraver, wrote about the cyma curve in his book, *The Analysis of Beauty: Written with a View to Fixing the Fluctuating Ideas of Taste.*

*These dramatic wood figures dating from the XIX Dynasty, circa
1303–1290 B.C., are still within reach at $400 and $500.*

"There is hardly a room," wrote Hogarth, "where one does not
see the waving line (of the cyma curve) employed in some way or
other. . . . Though all sorts of waving lines are ornamental when
properly applied, yet, strictly speaking, there is but one precise
line properly to be called the line of beauty." He then went on to

describe a style of Queen Anne chair which has come to be known as the Hogarth chair in which there are eighteen cyma curves in various degrees of exactness.

The cyma curve is a double waving line, convex at the top, and concave at the bottom. When the curves are reversed, concave at the top and convex at the bottom, it is called the cyma reversa. Another name, used indiscriminately for both but most properly for the cyma curve, is "ogee." The word ogee is the one we are most likely to encounter in furniture descriptions.

There is another vast and difficult to define area known by the French term, *objets de vertu.* Webster's definition seems to have little in common with popular usage of the term in the field of antiques. In auction catalogues, objets de vertu are usually small pieces often of exquisite workmanship, in gold, silver or other metal, sometimes employing semiprecious or even precious stones. Such objects often reach extremely high prices. An early Louis XV enameled gold snuffbox by a goldsmith named Noel Hardivillers sold not long ago at Christie's in London for $99,750. Another similar category is called "vinaigrette" which are not, as one might suppose, oil and vinegar holders for the dining room table, but small boxes, usually of precious metal, with pierced tops, designed to hold smelling salts. Articles made by Fabergé, who worked for the court of the Czars before the Russian Revolution, such as his jeweled Easter eggs and miniature trees fashioned of semiprecious stone with leaves of jade and blossoms of various-colored minerals, are true objets de vertu.

To give a more practical foundation to the foregoing, let us look at the area of oriental art to see what is being offered on the market today and what is being bought at relatively modest prices.

Almost since the day Thomas Edison invented the light bulb, Chinese porcelain and pottery vases have been used as lamp bases. You will find them at virtually every auction sale of home furnishings and in most antique shops. Their variety is endless, their beauty compelling, their shades often atrocious. Generally they are nineteenth- or twentieth-century copies of traditional shapes, decorations, finishes, and colors. They are mounted in brass stands; their bottoms are drilled for the fitting that holds the light socket and shade; and they were made to be used as lamp bases. But occasionally old vases of great value have been fitted as lamps, often with a rod bent to conform to the vase shape to avoid damaging the porcelain by drilling it. It is wise when you have bought such a

Fine porcelains are highly decorative wherever they are displayed in the home. This is how one collector showed his best pieces of eighteenth- and nineteenth-century English and Continental porcelain.

vase to remove the base on which it is mounted and examine the bottom for marks. A better auction house will do this for you and give the period of the piece, if it is old, adding "now mounted as a lamp." But in the lesser sales this is a neglected chore.

It is useless to try to describe the great variety of shapes and palettes that characterize Chinese vases of porcelain, not to mention the bronzes and pottery pieces and cloisonné that are also used as lamps. It is an enriching experience to go to the nearest art-book store, or to the public library, and look through a well-illustrated book on oriental porcelains. It is useful to know that almost every shape and style of decoration has been reproduced century after century since the days of the Mings, and if you see a rare beauty you would love to own, it is not unlikely that you will one day come across a not so rare copy. Sometimes the marks on the bottom of early Chinese porcelains have been reproduced as faithfully as the decorative pattern on its body, and without a practiced eye or the guidance of an expert, it is often difficult to tell the old from the new. In the catalogue of a well-run auction house, one will see the phrase "Ch'ien Lung six character mark, and of the period." Even in the eighteenth century, older pieces were copied, along with their marks, particularly pieces from the K'ang Hsi period which are of great beauty. The French imported many vases of the seventeenth and eighteenth centuries and mounted them in rich settings of gilded bronze as decorative pieces. This, too, is a fancy that has been copied to the present day, although the later and contemporary ormolu-mounted Chinese porcelains have a garishness about them that the earlier ones happily lacked.

Not long ago I bought a Chinese bowl in a small antique shop because the calligraphy scattered across its outer surface intrigued me, and I had never before seen a piece similarly decorated with peach blossom cloud shapes. The paste was of a peculiar grayish tone and I had no reason to assume that the six-character Ch'ien Lung mark on the bottom was authentic, as the price tag was $25. Since then I have shown it to someone more expert who assures me it is and that the piece has a minimum value of $500.

The world of oriental objects includes a vast range of bronzes—bits of archaic tools and weapons, often with a fine patina and encrustations of earth; small jade objects whose value can vary enormously; the tiny and often exquisite Japanese ivory and wood carvings known as netsuke (pronounced net-skee), usually representing figures from Japanese myths and fables. Sometimes these

This is a Peruvian human-effigy jar dating from the eleventh–fifteenth centuries. The strap held by the figure's hands supports a bag on its back, a carrying method still in use. It brought $600.

articles have great value. Until 1970, a netsuke was never known to have reached $2,000. Recently one sold in London for $27,000. Often seemingly unimportant little pieces of this kind can be picked up for a few dollars at a small auction or among the bits of flotsam in the dusty cases of a little antique shop.

The more unusual an object is, the more difficult it may be to identify its purpose or its origin, the more likely it is that you will find examples at low prices while poking through an auction or in your rounds of the antique shops.

Until recently, at least, Japanese weaponry was in this category —particularly sword guards and various other fittings once worn by

The standing figure with rudimentary arms and legs and exaggerated-head shape stamps this as a Protoclassic figure from the period 100 B.C., probably made in Jalisco, Mexico. It sold for $550.

the Samurai. Now there has been a surge of interest in weaponry of all kinds and an increase in the sophistication of collectors possibly stemming from interests first roused among soldiers stationed in Japan who brought home quantities of such objects in their loot. Even though interest in collecting such things has increased, they can still be found at low prices.

It must be repeated over and over again that the world of oriental objects is vast, much too broad and complex to be dealt with even in a whole volume, let alone in a section of one chapter of a book. The unschooled person should only assume that almost anything of oriental origin that he comes across, that pleases him be-

Primitive art has been rising steadily in value. This animal-head mask from the Bobo tribe of Upper Volta in Africa sold for $700.

cause of its shape, color, or workmanship, even carved ebony or ivory chopsticks, is a legitmate object of art.

Such objects are not limited to China and Japan. They come from every corner of Asia and its islands, from Thailand, Malaya, India, Korea—in short, from all parts of the Far East. Korea is particularly rich in pottery and porcelain whose importance to collectors is growing daily. Fabrics from the Far East should not be

Among nineteenth-century objects that turn up in little antique shops are Persian lacquer pen cases like the one above that brought $3,700 at auction. Only the most knowledgeable dealer would recognize that they have such great value.

overlooked. Old pieces of batik from India, and the beautifully embroidered old kimonos and mandarin coats from China and Japan are highly decorative.

Jade and other hard stones comprise an area that is seldom fully understood. It should come as no surprise that jade has a range extending from gem quality comparable in value to fine emeralds and other precious stones to a dull, gray-white stone that goes under the unprepossessing name of "muttonfat" jade. Singularly enough, objects carved out of muttonfat jade and its close cousin, white jade, are particularly sought after by collectors, especially the Orientals.

The value of jade objects varies according to the quality of the stone, in which color and translucency are considerations, and the quality of workmanship. This may depend upon the use the artisan has made of splashes of color in the stone to accentuate features of his carving—for instance, by carving a bird's plumage out of the mottled reddish-brown area of an otherwise white stone. The presumed age of the piece, which the workmanship often reveals to the practiced eye, is also important.

Though not nearly so popular, nor so highly valued even by Japanese collectors, Japanese porcelains have great beauty and can be found in a wide range of styles and price levels. Here are some typical Japanese porcelains, sold at Christie's in London at prices which ranged from a low of $26 to a high of $21,525.

The $26 item was:

Lot 62. A pair of Satsuma globular vases standing on four feet decorated in gold, green beige, and other colours with flowers, the shoulders with gilt scrolling handles—10¾ inches (27.5 cm.) high.

The item that brought $21,525 was:

Lot 181. A very fine Arita pear-shaped vase with short cylindrical neck, enameled in the Kakiemon style with overlapping rectangular panels of wisteria, plum, and bamboo branches on an iron-red net pattern ground, the neck with metal band and attached lacquer stopper—8½ in. (21.5 cm.) high.

Between those two extremes was a broad range of porcelain objects that brought under $100, and an even larger number that sold for between $100 and $200. In almost any collection of oriental porcelain there will be attractive pieces at prices the average person can afford, just as there were in this sale, held in the impressive surroundings of one of the world's great auction establishments.

CHAPTER

15

ANTIQUES FOR EVERYDAY DINING

IN THE DINING ROOM any lingering doubts you may have about buying antiques will be stilled. For here the widest price differences between the old and the new occur—in all aspects of table settings, including fine silver, porcelains, and glass.

The realm of objects for use makes even more pronounced the differences between the needs of the collector, with his emphasis on matters of authenticity and antiquity, and those of the homemaker whose guides are no more than beauty and quality. The collector, for instance, would want a fine set of Georgian silver that could cost many thousands of dollars to grace his table at special dinner parties. To go with his eighteenth-century service and eating utensils, he might want a set of twelve matched sterling service plates, which can run from a low of $500 each to a high of perhaps as much as $2,500.

Anything less than a set of four matched Georgian candlesticks would be inappropriate on a table set with such a service and these could cost as much as $5,000–$10,000 today. Then, too, he would need a pair of wine coolers in which to chill the champagne, preferably made by Paul de Lamerie or Paul Storr, and these might run him $10,000–$15,000. A silver tureen and tray by one of those makers, with matching covered vegetable dishes and meat platters of massive eighteenth-century sterling, could run $35,000–$50,000.

Fine eighteenth-century Worcester, Derby, or Sèvres porcelain would be a requirement for such a table, though perhaps a collector might prefer a set made in China in the eighteenth century, bearing the coat of arms of an English lord and his lady, or for a Yankee trader, bearing his most impressive clipper ship in full sail as the focus of its decoration. And as a centerpiece, a pair of porcelain pheasants from the reign of Ch'ien Lung in eighteenth-century China, or perhaps a seventeenth-century silver grouse from Augsburg, Germany?

The table covering? Lace, of course. Old *pointe de Venise*, its ecru thread further darkened by age, or Vincennes, or any one of a hundred different varieties and patterns of lace. With napkins of linen so fine it feels like silk.

The crystal would probably be contemporary. Matched sets of eighteenth-century glassware simply do not exist, although individual pieces from as far back as the seventeenth century are still to be found—beakers from Germany or Bohemia and even stemware from England. Baccarat is one of the finest makers of classic crystal today. Each place setting of contemporary copies of classic forms—white wines, Burgundy balloons, champagnes, desserts, cognac snifters—could cost as much as $200.

A lovely picture, but obviously not for us. Our sights are aimed somewhat lower. But let us see how close we can come to approximating such a gracious table within the limits of our middle-class pocketbooks.

First, the silver. Price today's sterling five-piece place setting at a good department store or jewelry shop. At the Tiffany level, which is close to the top, the range is from $108 to $199 for the basic five pieces—dinner knife, fork and cream-soup spoon, teaspoon and salad fork. At the mass produced level, the top price is $110 for a five-piece setting. At Fortunoff's, a chain of suburban bridal and gift shops in the New York, Long Island, and New Jersey area, a service of Gorham silver for twelve, with three serving pieces, runs from $1,250 to $1,500. Under almost any circumstances, you can judge that a service for twelve in sterling is going to cost above $1,000, and the cheaper it is, the lighter it will be in terms of weight. These lighter pieces often lack that substantial, solid heft that sterling is meant to have in the hand.

Now let us look at what we would have to expect at an auction sale, either an estate sale of all the possessions of one family, or a silver sale at a major auction house. At a good auction, the number of pieces in a set is stated, as well as the weight of the silver. Weighable silver excludes knives or other pieces with weighted handles. But weight is important, more so than the number of pieces in the set, and few sets are as small as the basic sixty-three pieces that cost a minimum of $1,000 when new.

What makes weight important is the price of silver as a commodity traded on world markets. If you look at the financial pages

Part of an assembled set of English flatware, dating mainly from the first half of the nineteenth century, by various London silversmiths, which brought $2,100 at auction. In spite of the set's very real antique value, the average cost for 268 ounces of silver was around $8.00 an ounce.

of your local newspaper, the chances are you will find a table that gives current prices of commodities and metals. As this is being written, silver in the New York market is past its peak price and has settled around $5.00 an ounce.

Keep that price—$5.00 an ounce—well in mind if you are shopping for silver. For at auction sales, the value of the silver content, if melted down and sold as ingots, is the primary factor in setting price levels. In most cases, sterling silver of no antique value sells at prices around its melt value. Modern pieces with decorative as well as utility value will run higher.

If an auction house does not weigh the silver, but only gives the number of pieces, forget for the moment that some are heavy serving pieces. You can assume that, in most cases, prices will run from

RICHARD A. BOURNE, INC.

A 102-piece set of Reed & Barton Francis I sterling flatware, including important serving pieces, which was sold at auction for $800.

$6.00 to $7.50, with some exceptional services bringing as much as $10 a piece. Weight was the ruling factor a decade ago when silver was much lower on the world market, and services were bringing $2.00 to $3.00 a piece. It is true today and will be true tomorrow, the price per piece and the price per ounce of silver rising and falling with the world market.

The reason for this is that most homemakers looking for silver have a particular style in mind, or they worry about engraved initials, or they just don't know such a vast price difference exists. As a result, most of the buyers of silver at auction are dealers and melt

A rare American silver tankard bearing the mark of Paul Revere and valued at $60–$80,000. It weighed just under 38 ounces.

value is the name of the game to them, the basic cost on which they figure their profit.

The proof of the pudding in this case is any auction catalogue with silver in it.

For example, here is a Los Angeles sale at Sotheby Parke Bernet. "English and Continental Silver, Property of the late Baroness von Wrangel and other owners." She could be the widow of the Russian general whose father was an arctic explorer and who fought the Bolsheviks in the Russian Revolution. Much of the Continental silver probably came from her collection.

This silver sauceboat and stand by The Gorham Company, circa 1900, sold at auction for $1,100.

Let's see now. German silver cup, Austrian silver liqueur set, Polish silver candlesticks. They sound like the Baroness. Here is a French silver service of 148 pieces from Charles Christofle et Cie., a firm that still does business in Paris a block from the Place de la Concorde. It is a service for twenty-four plus eight serving pieces in a black shagreen case with a brass handle and key. The weight is 238 ounces, not counting the knives. The price? $1,100. Excluding the eight heavy serving pieces, the price per setting would come to under $40 for what could be a seven- or eight-piece place setting.

Another. Service for eighteen, 168 pieces. Austrian silver by Thomas Dub, Vienna, 1885. With ice cream spoons, salt spoons, demi-tasse spoons, and other little niceties in addition to the usual place setting; six ladles, asparagus tongs, even knife rests. Weight:

An American silver tea and coffee service by Peter Chitry, circa 1820, brought $1,100.

213 ounces (excluding the knives). The price? $1,500, averaging $7.00 a piece or $35 for the conventional five-piece setting—less if we remember that heavy serving pieces were included in the $7.00 a piece price.

Another Austrian service for twenty-four, of 314 pieces including fourteen serving pieces and weighing 449 ounces. Price? $6.75 per piece, $35 a setting, $2,100 for the 314 pieces.

One other example in English silver. A large assembled service, 291 pieces, in the classic king's pattern, weighing 466 ounces. At the melt value of $5.00 an ounce, the set would be worth $2,330 to a dealer. It brought $2,400, or $8.00 a piece, $40 a place setting.

Or domestic services. International Sterling, the Wedgewood pattern, a big set of 171 pieces, probably twelve-piece place settings with ice tea spoons, grapefruit spoons, oyster forks, and other luxuries, 163 ounces of weighable silver, $900, or $5.25 a piece! A Gotham service in the Wheat pattern, service for twelve, 95 pieces, 104 ounces, $550.

Now one very special set. A large French silver-gilt service by G. Keller of Paris, made in 1900. Service for twenty-four with everything imaginable, 454 pieces in all, including four pairs of ice servers among the thirty-three serving pieces. Weight 759 ounces. The melt value would have been $3,795, but this was silver gilt and very beautiful, with high decorative value. It sold for $4,250, an average of only $9.35 per piece or $50 for a conventional five-piece place setting.

In any sale there can be two bidders who have their hearts set on one silver service for a daughter who is getting married. It is monogrammed. Letter M. One family is named Martinson, the other Miller. Both know the safest way to monogram silver for a daughter getting married is with her maiden name—just in case the silver has to serve through two or three husbands. She can always say it was her grandmother's service, particularly if it is old. Both want the set desperately. So the price will go up. But probably not to anywhere near what it would cost at Macy's.

But if you are bidding against a dealer and can afford to go one or two bids above melt value—the weight in ounces times approximately $5.00, which is where the dealers will stop bidding—the silver will probably be yours.

And if you cannot afford sterling, but balk at the inevitably slightly greasy feel of stainless steel, there is always silver plate. Not so long ago, services of silver plate went for around fifty cents a piece at an auction. Now the minimum is around $1.00 with the top at $1.35 a piece, just about double the cost of stainless, and to many people it would be well worth the difference. If the plating is worn off in spots, having them resilvered is a modest cost and only by looking at the markings could the pieces be distinguished from sterling.

When we move on to the large pieces another element enters the picture—decorative value. Melt value goes out the window in most cases, except for another very rough rule of thumb—decorative value is double melt value if there is no antique value to consider. But even at double melt, the price is far below the cost of new, decorative pieces and the choice is rich and almost endless.

What is true of silver is equally true of porcelain and glassware;

A pair of Derby sauce tureens, covers and stands, circa 1815, which would grace any table, brought $1,100 at auction.

Pieces from a Spode apple-green dessert service, circa 1816, some pieces of which were missing, sold at Sotheby Parke Bernet for $1,100.

Fine antique porcelain is not always out of reach. This Champion Bristol fluted part tea service, circa 1775, of which some pieces were damaged, sold for $400.

again we are speaking of pieces made in this century with no antique value. Handsome, rich-looking service plates and dinner plates can be found for around $10 each. Full services for twelve of porcelain, from good factories, in popular designs, always with a piece or so missing—eleven salad plates, nine cups, and ten saucers, etc.—can be acquired at attractive prices. Often the patterns can still be filled in, probably at prices that on the one hand will stagger you and on the other make you preen yourself at the good buy you had made originally.

Always a good buy is a set of silver holders and saucers for demi-tasse, consommé, and cream soups, with some of the porcelain liners missing. Often they go at modest prices because many people do not realize that the missing Lenox liners can be filled in at almost any good shop. And they do dress up a table.

If you are old-fashioned enough to like table linen, there is a bonanza awaiting you in bundles of fine double damask cloths and napkins—banquet size if you like—or lace tablecloths and lace-trimmed napkins. They are no bargain if you plan to have them laundered on the outside. But if you are up to the work of keeping them ready for the occasional dinner, you will find you can buy as much as you can carry.

The current popularity of pressed glass for table decorations makes it possible to bridge the gap between the contemporary and the antique. Pressed glass in classical patterns, made in the late nineteenth and early twentieth centuries, is relatively plentiful and much more affordable than many other antiques. Then, too, it is one technique that is strictly American in its origins.

Until an anonymous mechanic in the Sandwich, Massachusetts, plant of Deming Jarves perfected a technique in 1826 for pressing molten glass into a mold, the art of glassmaking had not changed since the first inventive Egyptian, Persian, or Chinese discovered, around 2000 B.C., that the pressure of the lungs passing through a four-foot pipe into a ball of molten sand and other earths resulted in interesting hollow shapes.

The earliest settlers brought glass blowers with them to this country. In Jamestown, Virginia, an English beadmaker named William Norton imported six Venetian experts to make glass beads for trading with the Indians. Glassmaking was started in Salem, Massachusetts, in 1638, and a few years later in New Amsterdam, the Dutch colony that became New York. German glassmakers were important in the founding of the industry—Caspar Wistar, John Greiner, Henry William Stiegel—as were Dutch, Italians, Swiss, and Bohemians.

More than just the techniques of glass blowing were handed down from the earliest recorded times. There is a remarkable similarity between early forms of glass produced in this country, probably by Italians, and early Roman glass. The Metropolitan Museum has a fish flask made in America in the nineteenth century and an almost identical flask from the days of the Roman Empire.

Glass factories were established primarily for the purpose of making window glass. Table glass and other objects were made originally by workmen using leftover metal (as the molten glass is called) to turn out bottles, flasks, and table glassware for their own homes and for their friends. A trade for glass objects developed later, as the population and demand grew.

Henry Stiegel established a glassworks at Mannheim, Pennsylvania, not far from Lancaster; Wistar established his factory on the banks of Alloway Creek in New Jersey, near Philadelphia. There were glassworks at Glassboro, New Jersey, Frederick, Maryland, Geneva, Pennsylvania, and scattered elsewhere all through

If a pair of candelabra like these should turn up missing a few prisms, there is still a good chance that matching pieces can be found. This one, which looks intact, sold for $650. It is Scandinavian, late eighteenth century.

the young colonies. Most of the enterprises flourished briefly as the immediate, adjacent demand was met, then died mainly because there was as yet no mechanism for distributing their products. Until the technique for pressing glass was established, they turned out a wide variety of blown-glass products—bottles, pitchers, flasks, wine and water glasses in various shades of blue, ranging from the palest turquoise to deep cobalt (Stiegel glass), amber deepening to brown, amethyst and red. For decorative wear, cut glass, made by pressing heavy lead crystal against grinding wheels to cut the pattern, was made until pressed glass was perfected and became the vogue. Pressed glass can easily be distinguished from cut glass because the lines of its patterns are soft as compared with the sharp edges of cut glass.

Pressed-glass table decorations can be found readily in shops and at auctions, at prices that are quite modest. This writer recently bought a late nineteenth-century set consisting of a pair of candle-sticks and a graceful fruit bowl for under $200. Individual pieces—pitchers, vases—can be found at prices under $100. Glass compotes and fruit dishes are also plentiful at modest prices.

Now we must look at some furniture to hold all this lovely silver, porcelain, and glass. We'll look at a Washington auction catalogue that has a plentiful supply of American and English pieces.

The big items first, starting with the sideboard, to set the dominant style. There are three in the catalogue—an "Antique Bow-Front Hepplewhite Mahogany" sideboard with satinwood inlay, $650; an "Antique Regency Inlaid Mahogany" sideboard, $190; and an "American Sheraton Mahogany Modified D-shape sideboard," $100.

Making a blind choice from that selection is difficult. The Hepplewhite piece at $650 sounds by far the most stylish and attractive with its satinwood inlay. And the price surely is not much for such an important piece. It may be that the availability of chairs will make the choice obvious.

In this sale there is only one set—"Twelve Antique Sheraton Mahogany Upholstered seat" chairs, two arm, ten side, $800. Without having seen either the chairs or the sideboards, it would appear that the American Sheraton mahogany piece would be the best choice, even though the price, $100, suggests that it may be in need of considerable work to bring it into usable condition. The chairs are certainly a bargain. Generally dining chairs with any age at all run at least $100 each. A set of twelve is a lot, which may be why the price was so low, since it takes a big dining room to accommodate that many chairs. But extra chairs can always stand against the wall of another room, even an upstairs bedroom.

A dining table is a problem. There is only one in the sale and it's the wrong wood. But there is a hunt table, late eighteenth or early nineteenth century, the description says, with a serpentine front, 88 inches long, 29 inches wide, 33 inches high.

That hunt table can be a trap, and you have to think long and hard before you can command the resistance to turn it down at $725, which looks like a bargain for a good antique. But turn it down you must unless you have a dining room big enough for a dining table and a hunt table at the opposite end, under the two little windows. You cannot have a dinner party at a table 29 inches wide and 88 inches long. Your guests (and no more than four of them would fit at such a table) would all be sitting crowded along one side facing across the table into the room as though at a dais with no audience. Or you would have to stagger their places since you could not have two dinner places opposite each other in that width with room between them for anything else. So reject the hunt table, please, except as a decorative piece in the library, where it can be moved easily to the terrace to serve as an outside bar for summer cocktails.

The next sale by the same house, Weschler of Washington, offers suitable alternatives. An American Hepplewhite mahogany dining table, circa 1800, 64 inches long when open, for $200—that's room for eight, as many as we're likely to have at a sit-down dinner in our little dining room. Fine. Wrap it up. Hepplewhite will go well with the Sheraton chairs. We'll take it.

What else do we need? Something on the other wall, opposite the sideboard, a serving piece. How about an "Antique Queen Anne Mahogany Tilt-Top Tea Table" that brought $375? It can stand against the wall with its top tilted when not in use and can hold extra things during a meal.

How much have we spent on this second most important room in the house? Sideboard $100, chairs, $800, table, $200, tea table, which we can almost use as a small dining table when there are no guests, $275. Total: $1,475. Add another $100 for cleaning and polishing the sideboard, an average charge. If we bought the Hepplewhite sideboard at $650 to match the table, instead of the Sheraton piece to go with the chairs, we still would have spent only $2,125. For a very handsome dining room.

16

WALK SOFTLY IN THE CARPET BAZAARS

So VAST, rich, and varied is the realm of rugs and carpets, that a person with limited resources as well as one with millions to spend can find exquisite floor coverings to complete the decor of a room. Rugs and carpets can be hung on the walls as one would hang a fine painting. They can be draped over furniture and, although often they are works of art of great value, even laid down to walk upon. They can be thick and furry with a pile an inch or more in depth, or have no pile at all. They can be woven of wool taken only from the breasts of the sheep where the natural oils have had the maximum protection from sun and rain, or of the softest camel hair. They can be light as the silk from which some of the finest are woven. Their colors can range the spectrum from black to snowy white. Their designs can tell a story, paint a picture, recite the history of a time. They comprise a sector of art so filled with complexities as to be bewildering unless we approach them from a somewhat simplistic perspective.

We tend to lump together as "oriental rugs" every kind of woven floor covering from the hills of Montenegro eastward to the China Sea. Rugs and carpets from what can roughly be defined as the Middle East—from Turkey through Afghanistan—are called "Turkey carpets" by the English with the same fine disdain for distinction that enables them to label all Bordeaux red wines as "claret" and all white wines from the Rhine Valley as "hocks." The term "Turkey carpets" has, at least, the saving grace of differentiating them from the Chinese, which we tend not to do.

First, the difference between rugs and carpets. Here the English do differentiate, and they are responsible for the accepted definition of a rug as a woven piece smaller than roughly 6 by 9 feet, and a carpet as anything larger. Two other sizes should be distinguished: runners and kelleyes. Runners are long narrow pieces, useful not only in hallways, on stairs, and in foyers, but handsome running the length of a room flanked by carpets and rugs of other shapes. Carpets that are approximately twice as long as they are wide are called kelleyes, a word that appears in neither Webster nor Oxford.

It is generally understood that rugs and carpets from the Middle East, what we speak of as orientals, can be and often are precious objects. Prices for antique carpets can range upward into the tens of thousands of dollars. But there are still a few new carpets arriving on our shores that are woven with the same care, by the same traditional methods used in the seventeenth and eighteenth centuries, the same designs colored with the same vegetable dyes, that also can run into five figures.

What makes a true oriental is the fact that its threads are hand-knotted and the rug is woven by hand. The different types of knots used are of importance only to one who really wishes to study the art of carpet weaving. But the size of the knots is important as a factor in quality, wear, and consequently, price. The finer the knot, the more knots to the square inch, the more threads, the closer the weave, the sturdier the carpet, the more precise the design—the longer the carpet will wear. If you look at the backs of a number of different orientals you will very quickly gain an impression of what a finely or loosely woven carpet looks like.

Many carpets described as orientals today are machine woven and colored with chemical rather than natural dyes. The quality of machine-made can be quite high and they can wear quite well. But they can also be poor imitations of the real orientals and should not be bought at oriental prices. Pakistan is copying rugs from every part of the Middle East, often using cheap rayon rather than wool or silk, and any contemporary carpet from Pakistan should be looked upon with suspicion.

As it was in antiquity, Persia—now called by its ancient name, Iran—is the heart of the industry today. The few fine new carpets that come on the market costing $10,000 or more are being made by hand in Iran employing age-old techniques. Until the oil-price boost, Iran's exports of rugs and carpets ran a not too distant second to the volume of its oil sales, and carpets are still an important export commodity.

From the days of antiquity the finest Persian carpets were the product of child labor. Groups of children with slender, nimble fingers worked under the watchful eye of a master rug weaver who had memorized the number of knots of each color needed to make a specific pattern. The children earned a few cents a day, the master weaver a few dollars. It could take months to make a large rug with five hundred knots to the square inch.

Now the Shah of Iran has ruled that Iranian children must go to school and the number of hours a day available for rug weaving has been drastically reduced. As a result, fewer rugs of the finest quality are being produced and more adult labor is being used, meaning higher labor costs and, inevitably, larger knots made by bigger fingers.

For our purposes there are six different kinds of carpet we should know about, and Persian carpets head the list.

A carpet does not have to be a Kirman to be good, although Kirmans on any list of used carpets generally are priced in the higher range. Indeed, taste is changing and the Kirmans, which are rather busy in their design, are losing some of their appeal to Americans. Persian carpets tend to be large and expensive, with floral designs rich in birds and animals that were doubtless part of the inspiration for Art Nouveau. Simpler patterns and colors such as the Khorassan carpets from the Meshed area of northeastern Iran are rising in desirability in this country.

Next in popularity (and familiarity) among Americans are the Bokharas from what is known as the Turkoman area of Central Asia. But here, too, changing tastes are affecting the demand for these carpets, distinguished by the generally red ground and patterns of octagons in various colors known as "elephants' feet." In this group are the Afghans, also red, although many are now bleached with chemicals for the American market and are known as "golden Afghans."

Third are the carpets from the Caucasus, with geometric designs in greens, yellows, blues, and shades of brown—Kubas, Daghestans, Derbends, Shirvans, Chichis. Often these are kilims, carpets woven without a pile, which can be durable nonetheless; or so-called Soumacs which, like kilims, have no pile but also have an unfinished look on the back with loose threads like a needlepoint rug. Although there is no real similarity, the Caucasus rugs often give an impression not unlike that of an American Navajo rug.

Fourth are the Anatolian carpets, recognized by a cherry-red ground with a design of large and small medallions. These rugs include many of the dramatic prayer rugs from Giordes, Ladik, and

Bergama. They are infinite in their variety of design and color, as well as materials, and are much sought after by collectors.

Coming back into favor are the Chinese carpets, patterned with all the symbolism that characterizes Chinese porcelains—the lotus, vases of flowers, fish, dragons, on grounds of deep blue, pale yellow, salmon, burnt orange, and in natural wool colors. Many older Chinese carpets that were woven in strong colors were bleached for the American market.

Sixth are Indian carpets being produced today in handmade and machine versions of Persian and Chinese designs and weaves, but still often using traditional Indian colors and designs typical of Indian art.

The range of prices on today's market for used rugs and carpets is wide, running from under $500 to well into the upper five figures. What concerns us is the bottom of this broad range and before we get into the buying of carpets we must ask ourselves some questions.

Assuming that we are not buying carpets as collectors, why do we want them?

For the color and warmth they lend a room, of course. For their decorative quality. Because they provide a pattern, whether they are room size or small rugs, that contrasts with the color of the floor itself, providing another focus for the eye. Because they are soft underfoot and an insulation against cold floors in winter.

Then why not wall-to-wall carpeting?

Wall-to-wall carpeting is fine if you have a room full of color and pattern and need a neutral tone with no distraction for the eye on the floor. But it adds little distinction to our antique furnishings and has no personality of its own.

Keep several cost factors in mind when you decide between wall-to-wall carpeting and area rugs. With the latter there is no waste—it covers a specific part of the floor. When you buy wall to wall you pay for an oblong or a square whose largest dimensions conform with the largest dimension of the floor you are covering. If the room size varies from the width of the carpet roll, you could have considerable waste. If there is an alcove, your wall to wall must go smoothly into that alcove, preferably without patching, and many small waste pieces of carpeting could be left over. When you move—and 25 per cent of the people in the middle-income range in the United States move every year—your oriental will move with you and will almost certainly be suited to the rooms in your new home. But the wall to wall can rarely be moved successfully and must be considered a total or almost total loss.

As for maintenance, it must be remembered that home carpet scrubbing equipment was developed to deal with the multifarious maintenance problems presented by wall to wall, not oriental carpeting. Wall to wall, unless it is of the very finest quality, is highly susceptible to stains and dirt. It pills, sometimes forever, giving up great gobbets of what look like dust balls but are, in fact, bits of the material of which the carpet is woven. This pilling often must be picked up by hand because no vacuum cleaner is capable of digesting it. We have even had to invent carpet rakes to pull these gobbets into a heap where they can be dealt with.

Orientals, on the other hand, mellow with time, taking on a patina that may eventually dull their colors to the point where they need to be washed. But then they can be sent out for cleaning and even for repair at a cost far below what would be involved in the regular scrubbing of wall to wall with bought or rented equipment.

At small auction sales, rugs and carpets will usually be piled in a heap at the exhibitions. If we want to look at a carpet near the bottom of a pile, we must find a porter or haul them about ourselves. A tip is a necessity if he has to move a number of carpets to get at one we want to examine in detail. Larger carpets may be rolled and tied and it is futile to try to have them unrolled in a crowded auction exhibition room. All we can do is to slow down the proceedings at the sale so we can look them over from the back if possible—where repairs and damage are most likely to show—before we put in our bids.

Once I paid $35 at a sale for a Chinese carpet. It was approximately seven by nine feet and so dirty I was not even sure what the color was, though it seemed to have a reddish ground. At home, a vigorous scrubbing with soap and water on an outside terrace revealed it to be of a magnificent magenta ground with clusters of flowers at the corners and the silky sheen of Chinese carpets made sixty years or so ago.

The carpet had, presumably, been walked on for most of those years. It was obviously not in perfect condition. The nap, which probably was an inch deep when it was made, was half that depth and in some places it was gone entirely so the backing threads showed through. But this hardly detracted from the carpet's beauty and usefulness. Remember the gracious French homes where we may see eighteenth-century chairs covered with tapestry of the period that is so worn in places the threads barely hold it together? It is quite reasonable to take the same attitude toward good carpets. It is no more a sign of poverty to have an old oriental carpet that is threadbare in places than it is to have a fine antique chair with worn fabric of the period.

Often we see advertisements from furniture or department stores that offer used oriental rugs and carpets and classify them as "excellent," "good," or "worn." Sometimes a carpet described as worn will bear a higher price tag than an excellent one of similar size and pattern made later. Antiquity and workmanship—the number of knots to the square inch, the kind of dye, the extent to which chemical bleaches may or may not have been used—would contribute to the difference in price.

Orientals are being merchandised today as a "good investment," and they are being bought new with the expectation that over the years, granted they are not damaged, they will at least retain their value if not, in fact, become more valuable. This is an iffy proposition and not one we should accept without examination. The argument used to promote new orientals as investments is that the methods of making them are changing because of the new laws governing child labor. Given my choice between a new carpet that sells for $10,000 today, and may indeed be worth it, and five carpets made at the turn of the century or even as late as 1915, in fine condition, which can be bought at even so prestigious a house as Sotheby's in London for around $2,000, I would buy the five rugs at $2,000, if only because they have doubled in value in the past five years and can be expected to continue to go up in price.

Coming down to our level—buying carpets to walk on, for their decorative value and not as investments or as collector's items—there are many possible choices. The deep red Bokharas and Afghans, as well as floral pattern Kirmans, are losing out as a matter of taste and are, therefore, not markedly going up in price. One auctioneer recently told me, "You can't give the reds away." That, of course, is an exaggeration. What it means is that good Bokharas and Afghans can be bought for a few hundred dollars today at almost any auction. Kirmans are still in this writer's opinion, high, but as the word spreads that decorators are passing them up, dealer competition for them will dissolve and they will move downward at a more perceptible rate than is apparent today.

What is taking their place are the carpets in soft tones of gold

The foyer of an apartment on New York's upper East Side furnished entirely with pieces from Sotheby Parke Bernet sales bought at modest cost. The Empire chest flanked by chairs in the Sheraton manner with a trumeau mirror above provide a perfect foyer grouping.

The great oval-shaped American dining-room table makes this room. It seats ten comfortably, and each person can see every other guest at the table. The chairs are left over from an earlier decor and are far too heavy. They will be replaced when just the right set of Queen Anne mahogany dining chairs comes along at an acceptable price.

WILLIAM DOUGLAS KING

WILLIAM DOUGLAS KING

The dining room of what was once a farmhouse on Long Island. The table is a late nineteenth-century reproduction of a George II original. The chairs are American Queen Anne ashwood, probably early nineteenth century. The set cost $240 at auction. The candlesticks are Louis XVI gilded bronze and were bought some years ago for $60. The pair of still lifes are nineteenth-century chromo lithographs in their original frames. The window shades were painted by hand by Ursula Sternberg of Elkins Park, Pa.

This extraordinary George II needlepoint carpet, 8 feet 3 inches by 5 feet 5 inches, decorated with various Chinese vases in blue and gold on a red ground, brought an extraordinary price, $8,750

A semiantique (50 to 100 years old) Malayer Sarouk rug sold by the Richard A. Bourne Gallery, Inc. for $700.

Semiantique Sarouk carpet which sold at auction for $900.

At the top of the price scale, for rich collectors only, this seventeenth-century Savonnerie carpet brought $150,000 at a New York sale.

and green and yellows and browns, the carpets with geometric designs from the Caucasus, the kilims and the Soumacs with no pile, the carpets that remind one of the Navajos. They are starting to go up, but are still good buys, and it is safe to say they will be good investments if that is a part of your interest.

There are a few rules to be observed in shopping for carpets.

The first step is of major importance—learning how to tell a handmade oriental from a cheap machine-woven imitation. Look at the border or any other repeated segment of design. If two seg-

Although prices for oriental carpets have gone sky-high, there are still pieces made in the early part of this century that are in good supply at acceptable prices. This Senna Kilim sold for $600.

ments are identical, you can almost bet that the piece was machine woven. Even the best master rug weavers miscounted or interrupted their work to chase the goats out of the wheat field, resulting in a break in the pattern.

The heavily merchandised auction sales often held on Sunday afternoons in the parlors of big city hotels are not the place to look for bargains. True the carpets they offer are clean and, when necessary, skillfully repaired. But such sales are often heavily larded with shills placed to keep the bidding going and to generate an air of excitement that can carry the innocent away. The few excellent

Kilim rugs and carpets, which are woven without a pile, are much in demand because they are less expensive than the more intricate weaves and wear extremely well.

antique carpets that are featured at these sales often are there only as eye-catchers and are likely not to be sold but rather knocked down to someone bidding for the house.

In buying the dirty carpets at a small house sale or other auction, keep in mind that you will likely have a cleaning bill and possibly even a bill for repairs.

Learn to look at the backs of carpets as well as at their finished surfaces. Do not be discouraged if you see signs of repairs on the back. If they are skillfully done and do not show on the front, the carpet may come to you more cheaply than if it were perfect and may still be as useful as a more expensive piece. Look at the fringes, particularly if they appear to be newer than the rest of the carpet. If this is the case, it may mean that a carpet has been cut down to remove a damaged portion, which also would reduce its value to a dealer, though not necessarily to you or to me.

Above all, read up a little bit on oriental carpets. There are several good books listed in the appendix. They will tell you more about carpets than can be dealt with in this space and will give you the courage you need to enter the competition for carpets at an auction sale.

CHAPTER

17

EXPERTISE AND FAKERY

"EXPERTS" and "appraisers" are one and the same in some countries but not in the United States. While an appraiser obviously should be an expert in the area in which he is making valuations, an expert need not necessarily be equipped to furnish exact market values. Prepare yourself to think of, and deal with, an appraiser separate from an expert unless you are fortunate enough to find an appraiser who happens to be expert in the area that concerns you.

Although the collector may have frequent occasion to consult with experts in various fields, at our level—the modestly priced, reasonably good piece of furniture, object or work of art being bought for our use—we would be more apt to seek out an appraiser. What we should know when we consult an appraiser and what we should expect and require of one can be terribly important.

Generally it is in the appraising of fine art—paintings or drawings in particular—that problems arise, since we are dealing here with unique items. The problem lies in establishing fair market value for something that is irreplaceable and almost never susceptible to comparison with a like work by the same artist except on a purely subjective basis.

In obtaining an appraisal, the appraiser would need from you the following information:

1. The name of the artist, school, period, or other attribution.

2. The title, if any, or a description if it is untitled.

3. The medium. In addition to whether it is painted in oil, watercolor, gouache, or drawn with crayon, pencil, pen and ink, or charcoal, list what it is painted or drawn on—canvas, panel, board— or if a drawing, the kind of paper and whether it is watermarked.

4. The dimensions, which means the height and width of the

painted or drawn surface, not the size of the paper or framing.

5. A photograph of the work, not necessarily in color, since color photographs are at best an approximation, and it is the composition and detail that are important. If a photograph is not available, then the fullest possible description should be provided the appraiser.

6. The provenance—where has it been before you acquired it? In short, a history of its ownership since it was created, if that is possible, or as far back as it is known. An important element in a provenance is any record of exhibitions at which the work has been shown and catalogued, any reproductions that have appeared in books or magazine articles.

7. The condition of the work. In the case of old masters, this might require an ultraviolet examination to determine whether there is any overpainting or other alteration in the original work.

On the basis of the information the owner provides the appraiser, he should be able to determine its fair market value, either from his own knowledge, if he is sufficiently expert, or through research in accepted sources. *Fair market value* itself requires definition. It is the price at which the property would change hands between a seller willing to part with it and a buyer willing to purchase it, free of any pressure or compulsion on either side and with both sides being fully aware of the relevant facts regarding the property.

Once the appraiser has arrived at a figure, he will adjust it to allow for the type of valuation being sought. If it is for insurance purposes, it is his duty to place the highest valuation possible, since what he is being asked to do is to set a value on something that is probably irreplaceable, in a market that is moving steadily upward.

If an appraisal is for estate purposes, that is, to be used as a valuation for the purpose of paying inheritance taxes, the problems are many and complex. The Internal Revenue Service scans very carefully fine art that is included in an estate, particularly in the case of pictures with a value of $10,000 or more. The IRS has grown to mistrust estate appraisals of art because of the difficulty of getting any two appraisers to agree on a valuation. It has, accordingly, chosen a committee of ten art experts to pass judgment on valuations on the basis of three options: either they regard the appraisal of a work as "clearly justified," or "questionable," or "clearly unjustified." The same is true in the case of valuations made for tax deductions resulting from gifts of works of art to nonprofit institutions. An exception would be where a valuation may be on the low side of the scale for inheritance tax purposes; and probably be on the high side for figuring the value of a charitable contribution for tax purposes.

Most of the recognized appraisers who specialize in the field of fine arts are highly competent, with backgrounds either as dealers, auctioneers, or long-time students of the field. Many dealers carry on appraisal work as a sideline, usually for their customers. The best yardstick for measuring the competence of an appraiser is his track record, if it is obtainable, under the scrutiny of government tax specialists or the courts.

Just as this is a country of vast riches in fine art, antiques, and objects of art, it is also rich in expertise. There are experts in this country on every style, period, technique of the plastic arts and artisanship, just as there are expert restorers who can rebuild a thin place on a sixteenth-century drawing paper, or put together a shattered Greek krater, or mend a fourteenth-century painting whose wood panel has cracked and split right through the madonna's face.

Anyone who has read about the Metropolitan Museum's shattered million-dollar Greek krater must realize that damage to a piece does not necessarily make it valueless. The Met's krater was in pieces when it was bought and had to be given to an expert restorer to be put together. Auction catalogues that provide prospective bidders with full information often mention repairs. Even a lowly piece of eighteenth-century faïence from France may be offered for sale, though it is cracked and riveted, and can command a respectable price.

Rarity is, of course, the decisive factor here. The Chinese have always gone to exquisite lengths to protect rare, delicate pieces of porcelain and other objects. A fine Chinese piece will frequently be offered with a case that has been made for the piece, its interior padded and lined with silk to fit the precise form. Such pieces were seldom left out on display but were kept in chests to be opened and shown to deserving guests or to be admired and handled only by their owners. Even so, oriental pottery does not necessarily lose its value because it is chipped or broken. This is particularly true, of course, of funerary pieces that have been buried for centuries and have lost most of their decoration through the chemical action of the soil.

You would, of course, consider repairs to a piece that has important sentimental value, if the cost does not seem prohibitive. But you should also consider repairing something you may buy in poor condition at a bargain price. Often such a piece can be sold later at a substantial profit.

There is a story that must be told here, even though it is not wholly apposite. An elderly Frenchman, once a man of great wealth who has become impoverished, is invited by an important family to the wedding of a daughter. He examines his dress clothes and finds that with a brushing and pressing they are still serviceable. He takes out his decorations dating from a happier day, to be worn on his chest. Then he begins the search for something worthy of the family's wealth as a wedding gift. Passing a little antique shop on the Left Bank he spots a shattered vase on a table just inside the door and asks if it is for sale. It is worthless, he is told, but he can have the pieces for ten francs. To this he adds another ten francs and instructs the shopkeeper to wrap it in its broken condition in a box of the size that would be needed if it were whole and to treat it as a gift.

At the wedding, he approaches the receiving line on a raised platform in the ballroom of the Ritz on the Place Vendome. As he mounts the stairs, holding his gift wrapped package, he stumbles and lets the package fall. A sigh of distress rises from the assembled guests. The bride reassures him that she values his gift, even though it may be broken, and opens it to see its condition—only to find that the antique dealer has wrapped each broken piece carefully in a separate sheet of tissue.

End of story.

How do you find an expert restorer? Most dealers know some, but museums are the best source of such information. A list of restorers in many parts of the country, along with their areas of experience, is included in the appendix at the back of this book.

Do not expect a restorer to finish a job overnight. Sometimes it will be months before he is satisfied with the results and is ready to surrender the repaired piece. Over the years restorers accumulate vast assortments of bits and pieces that can be used in repairs. Sometimes they have contact with other restorers with whom they trade for pieces they need to finish a job. Almost any old clock, watch, or automaton such as a canary that sings in a little cage, its movements controlled by a clock mechanism, can be restored so it works perfectly. This is true of music boxes, old toys, electric trains, and almost anything else you can think of that is collected.

Any piece of furniture can be restored to its original condition, even though delicate inlaid woods are missing. There are shops that deal in veneers of all kinds. This writer once found in such a shop, whose floor space was taken up with trays of all kinds of tiny pieces of veneer, large flitches, or sheets, of mahogany that had been bought from government surplus after World War I, and which I used to restore the paneling on the sides of a 1947 Town & Country convertible sedan. During the war the veneers had been used for fighter plane bodies.

Many restorers double as experts, as do dealers and appraisers. Again, museums are a useful source to locate a specific area of expertise. Often museum curators will offer an opinion as to the authenticity of a piece, but some museums prohibit this kind of activity by its employees.

Here a word must be said about fakes and forgeries. Through the ages there have been men who have felt frustrated because their talents or craftsmanship went unappreciated and have turned to the production of paintings, sculpture, furniture, silver, porcelain and, indeed, almost any object of value, utilizing techniques designed to make it possible to pass off their work as of a period or by a hand that gives them great value.

In dealing with paintings in Chapters 10 and 12, we touched on some of the problems created by legitimate artists that have contributed to much of the confusion regarding fakes and forgeries. There are some critics who call every copy of a painting a fake or a forgery, but this is an exaggerated view. Copies painstakingly made by professionals, who sit week after week in a museum carefully reproducing every minute detail on a famous painting, may have the signature of the artist who painted the original added by an unscrupulous owner later, even where the original bore no signature. These are certainly fakes, but it was not necessarily the intent of the copyist to produce a fake.

Intent is important here. Did the maker of the copy intend to pass it off as an original work? If so, it is a forgery. If not, it is a copy or a reproduction. The person who adds a signature or other identifying mark to such a piece intends to pass it off as an original, and thus it becomes a forgery.

Many years ago this writer bought at an auction a small attractive bronze bearing an authentic-looking Degas signature, as well as the seal of the Hebrard foundry that produced the great Degas sculptures. The price was modest, around $250 as I recall, and obviously the dealers present knew it was not by Degas. So did I. It was a centaur, and I knew well that while Degas had made sculptures of horses and humans, he had never been known to combine them in one piece. But I was curious and bought it. A letter to the Hebrard foundry brought the reply that the piece was known to them and had indeed emanated from its workshops. But it was the work of a little-known Parisian sculpture to which someone at a later date had added the Degas signature. Without the signature, it would probably be worth today several times the sum I paid for it. But the signature puts it into a gray area where its value is questionable.

Barring pieces on which such a signature has been added, we should take the pragmatic view, since we are buying for use, not as collectors. We accept good copies as reproductions, with fore-knowledge that this is what they are and with none of the uneasiness that comes when one is about to shell out a substantial sum for a work of art or artisanship that just might not be authentic.

Yet we may find ourselves confronted by a situation where a dealer assures us a piece of furniture is eighteenth century when in fact it probably is a nineteenth-century reproduction. Is the piece a fake? Not at all. The dealer may be a fake if he is asking a price commensurate with an eighteenth-century piece and knows it is a later reproduction. But if the price is reasonable and the piece is attractive and in good condition, is anyone being cheated?

If, however, we are about to take a plunge and buy one absolutely genuine piece of eighteenth-century furniture because we know that one such piece will upgrade, in the eyes of the beholder, the nineteenth-century reproductions in the same setting, then we should protect ourselves against misrepresentation. If the dealer is honest he will have no objection to writing out a bill of sale stating exactly what it is he is selling and you are buying. It should include a complete description of the piece, its period, style, decorative details, and any exceptions in period or style such as later hardware. It should state when (approximately) and where it was made. On the basis of such a bill of sale, it is possible to obtain redress if it can be shown that the piece is not as represented. But in such a case, all the dealer can be accused of is an honest mistake.

There is also the question of honest error in attributions. Every museum owns works, particularly old master paintings, which, as we have noted earlier, were seldom signed and on which attributions change from time to time as the level of scholarship in the particular field or even perhaps that of the museum itself improves.

"Aristotle with a Bust of Homer" by Rembrandt. From The Metropolitan Museum of Art, purchased with special funds and gifts of friends of the museum in 1961.

Recently the Metropolitan Museum of Art re-examined and changed the attributions on a number of paintings in its collection, downgrading them from works by acknowledged masters to the product of followers. The press raised a howl about fakes.

But they were not fakes, painted with the intent to deceive, or with the name of an artist added by a forger at a later date. They were pictures that were unsigned, on which the provenances—the history of the works—were scanty or nonexistent.

As an example, let us look at the history of the Rembrandt painting, "Aristotle Contemplating the Bust of Homer," from the Parke Bernet catalogue of the Erickson Collection sale in 1961, at which it brought the sensational price, for the time, of $2,300,000. The description noted that it was signed on the base of the bust "Rembrandt f." and dated 1653. This was followed by a historical footnote and provenance:

Note. The genesis of this picture forms part of one of the most curious events of Rembrandt's life. In the 'fifties his popularity as a painter had declined sharply in Holland, and he was entering on a period of financial straits which culminated in the cession of his possessions to his creditors in July 1656, and the forced sale of his collection of paintings, including a number of his own works. Nevertheless, his fame had spread widely through Europe; and in 1652, Don Antonio Ruffo, a Sicilian nobleman of Messina, wrote to the painter and commissioned from him the present painting, which was completed in 1653 and delivered in the following year. It may be noted that the bust of Homer shown in the picture is mentioned in Rembrandt's own inventory; it was probably a cast of the original, which is in the Naples Museum.

In the Bolletino d'Arte, of 1916, appeared an extended study written by the Marquis Vincenzo Ruffo of the history of the vast collection of paintings once owned by his family; and from the surviving documents he published, among other historical material of the time, the full story of his ancestor's transactions with Rembrandt from which we extract the data which follow.

As indicated above, the painting . . . was delivered in 1654; the Marquis was so pleased with this work which was christened "Aristotle" that he decided to have two companion pieces executed by the Italian painters Guercino and Preti; and the former went so far as to paint for him "a Cosmographer" in which the subject is shown contemplating a globe, this being Guercino's concept of a suitable companion to Aristotle, which he took to represent a "phisiognomist."

The Marquis then changed his mind and decided to order the two additional paintings from Rembrandt himself; and the painter sent him in 1661 an "Alexander the Great" and in 1662 a "Homer," the latter of which was returned to be changed at the owner's request. The two last pictures dropped from sight during the ultimate dispersal of the Ruffo collections, and present authorities can only speculate on their identity with various known works (e.g. Dr. Bredius' "Homer" at The Hague, which is actually dated 1663, and is published by him as being the Ruffo picture). The last known appearance of the "Alexander" occurred when the collection as a whole passed in 1743 to a cadet branch of the family, owing to the death of the older members from the plague*; this picture was alienated from the estate and was sold at auction in Amsterdam on June 5, 1765.

Further details of interest concerning the "Aristotle" include the fact that the intermediary by which it was delivered was a certain Cornelius Eysbert van Goor of Amsterdam; the cost of the painting was five hundred florins, and of the packing, weighing, transportation, etc., fl. 15.85. The correspondence also indicates the manner in which the payments could be remitted, as prescribed by the agent van Goor. The painting was carried from Texel to Naples in the ship *Bartholomeus* and then transported from Naples to Messina.

The "Aristotle" seems to have left the Ruffo collection during the lordship of Don Giovanni, who became the head of the family about 1760; and it was already in the well-known collection of Sir Abraham Hume at the beginning of the nineteenth century. At this time, the history and title had become obscured, and it was known throughout the century under different titles (vide infra); as late as 1910, the subject was variously styled in the considerable Rembrandt literature.

After the footnote came the full provenance:

Painted for the Marquis Antonio Ruffo in 1652–53 (vide supra).

Collection of the Ruffo family of Messina, Sicily.

Collection of Don Giovanne Ruffo e la Roca, Messina, c. 1760.

Collection of Sir Abraham Hume, Bart., Ashbridge Park, Herts, before 1815.

Collection of Earl Brownlow, Ashbridge Park, Herts, his son-in-law.

---

* Thus the "Alexander the Great" according to present scholarship is a "lost" Rembrandt which may one day turn up at an obscure auction mislabeled, to be bought by someone with curiosity for a few hundred dollars. Ed.

Collection of Rodolphe Kann, Paris, cat. no. 65 (as "Portrait of a Savant").

From Duveen Bros., Inc., New York.

This was followed by a list of exhibitions in which the picture had been shown, catalogues in which it had been mentioned, and other literature in which it was described and reproduced.

Such is the scholarship that can go into the attribution of a painting to a specific artist. Lacking the kind of historical record provided by the Ruffo archives, the attribution of a painting becomes largely a matter of opinion. Science is called upon to examine a work for overpainting and to test its materials to determine whether the medium in which it is painted was in use at the time. Every brush stroke is examined and compared with other known works by the artist. The literature of the period is combed and recombed in the search for clues on the basis of which an attribution may be sustained.

Then later scholars come along and after a new study decide that the picture is not by, say, Frans Hals, but by a later artist who painted in the manner of Hals, perhaps in the late seventeenth century, but probably after Hals' death in 1666.

So the museum, which has shown the painting as by Hals, is faced with a distressing choice. It can ignore the later attribution, either because it has less faith in the later scholar than in the earlier one who put Hals' name to the work, or simply because it doesn't want to lose its only Hals by having it transformed overnight into a relatively unimportant work by a follower. Or it can weigh the evidence pro and con, then submit the work to another scholar or group of scholars of its own choice for further study, on the basis of which it may or may not change the attribution.

Unfortunately there are many of what may charitably be called errors of attribution hanging in American museums. During the late nineteenth and early twentieth centuries many wealthy Americans were badly deceived by unscrupulous European dealers into building collections of old masters, few of which were as described. Upon their deaths they left these works to museums which may only belatedly have learned how misled they and the donors were. This is one of the reasons why the market in old masters in the United States is poor—and why such a vast proportion of the paintings that come on the market here are bought by shrewd European dealers often for far less than they are worth.

There is, of course, another side to this coin. Works that have been considered unimportant may, as a result of better scholarship, be upgraded and receive firm attribution as by the hand of a great master.

As for what an authentic piece can do among lesser pieces, there is a story. A friend of this writer's (a Hungarian woman of great beauty who left Budapest by its western portals as the Russians entered it from the east) lives now in Washington, wife of a journalist, and was dressing one evening for a diplomatic ball. She had one good piece of jewelry, a pearl necklace, but felt it needed something more dramatic for such an event. In her home there was a crystal girandole (a candelabra hung with prisms) with a green glass bauble hanging from it. In a moment of happy inspiration she detached it and suspended it from her really good pearls.

At the ball, an old friend from better days in Budapest rushed up to her.

"My dear!" she exclaimed. "How wonderful! You saved your mother's emerald."

One word more on fakes. In his definitive book on the art of faking furniture, Herbert Cescinsky* points out that the population of Great Britain in 1800 was under 12 million, which, in that age of large families, meant that there were probably 2 million families. Of these he estimates that not more than 2,000 were able to afford to order furniture made by Chippendale from 1730 to 1790. He continues: "Yet, what these 2,000 families had made (by Chippendale and other cabinetmakers of the period) has equipped most of the millionaires homes and apartments from New York to the Pacific Coast, to say nothing of the huge stocks in the hands of American dealers. . . . What has been left has to be divided into what remains *in situ* (that is, in the stately English homes for which it was made) and the residue left to reinforce English dealers' stocks." Mr. Cescinsky goes on to make the point that "more is shipped to America in one year than could have been made in the whole of the eighteenth century."

So, if you should buy a piece of eighteenth-century English furniture and some self-styled expert among your friends should tell you that it is not of the epoch, be of good cheer.

You are probably in very good company.

*The Gentle Art of Faking Furniture, Herbert Cescinsky, Dover Publications, Inc., New York, paperbound.

18

THE OLD VERSUS THE NEW

MY Sunday newspaper regularly carries full-page advertisements of one of the big national furniture department stores which sells antiques, contemporary reproductions, and modern furniture and decorations of all kinds. One would not expect to find bargains in antiques in such a store. Yet they exist. In many cases pieces described as authentic—that is, of the period indicated by their style—sell for less than contemporary reproductions. Here are some examples from a recent advertisement:

A small Louis XVI love seat, a contemporary reproduction, regularly $995, on sale at $695.

A wing chair, no indication of style but again, a contemporary reproduction, $995, on sale at $795.

An Empire armchair, cherry finish, regularly $495, on sale at $325. Cherry finish means just that, finished to resemble cherry, the kind of wood not indicated.

A painted drop-leaf table $795, on sale at $495.

Now compare those prices with the prices of pieces described by the same store as genuine antiques:

A pair of George II chairs, circa 1740, regularly $695, on sale at $475.

A mahogany Chippendale chair, circa 1790, regularly $275, on sale at $175.

A Queen Anne side chair, circa 1720, regularly $450, on sale at $325.

Any of those pieces, if the dating is accurate, would be bargains even when compared with auction prices, something to keep in mind when you are shopping.

Larger pieces, all described as dating from the nineteenth century, by contrast run much higher and offer less value.

These corner chairs present an interesting contrast. The antique above, George I in elmwood, made in the first quarter of the eighteenth century, sold for only $900 at auction; the contemporary reproduction, on facing page, can be bought for just under $900.

A small English buffet, circa 1860, regularly $1,295, on sale at $895.

A green lacquer chest, circa 1860, $1,495, on sale at $1,195.

A set of six mahogany dining chairs, circa 1860, regularly $2,295, reduced for sale to $1,695.

Now, as a further contrast, let us look at the catalogues of two sales, #64 and #66, held at Sotheby Parke Bernet in Los Angeles and see if we can furnish another living room on our level—at a price under $3,000—for less than we would have to spend for new reproductions.

Let us assume that this is a good-sized room in a suburban home —say 16 by 24 feet. We'll start with a carpet, because that will determine our basic color scheme and we do not want to do a lot of

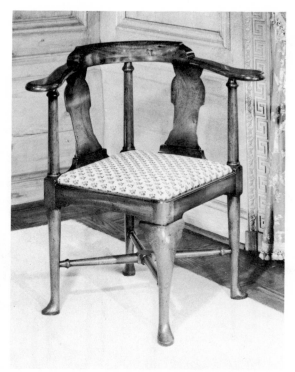

WOOD AND HOGAN, INC.

recovering if the upholstery on the pieces we buy is in good condition. We have an immediate choice of two Chinese carpets. Lot 12 in Sale ✕66 is a carpet 13 feet 6 inches by 10 feet, having a salmon pink field woven at the center with a flowering tree and a stylized pheasant with a border of meandering foliage.

The carpet brought $375—just $25 a square yard, less than you would pay today for good wool broadloom.

The second is Lot 15a, slightly smaller—11 feet 6 inches by 9 feet 3 inches, with a yellow field (an unusual color and it sounds lovely) woven with an urn of chrysanthemums amid sprigs of flowering branches and exotic birds, with a plum-colored border having scrolling foliage. It went for $650.

We'll settle for Lot 12, for reasons of price as well as size, and make a mental note that we've spent a little over 10 per cent of our budget for an important item in our room. But let's keep in mind

Two nests of tables. On facing page is a contemporary reproduction in mahogany with rosewood veneer tops by Kittinger, priced at $1,145. Above is an unusual Regency nest of five tables, dating from the first quarter of the nineteenth century, veneered in exotic woods including rosewood, satinwood, partridgewood, bird's-eye maple, and burr elm, rare because entire nests of this kind seldom survive intact. It was expected to bring $800 to $1,000 at auction. Instead, the set sold for $2,300.

a nineteenth-century Aubusson carpet, 7 feet 9 inches by 7 feet 4 inches, with a pale green-beige ground, a border of floral sprays and the four corners with ribbon-tied bouquets in tones of pink, blue, green, and yellow, $200, as a second carpet with the yellow, in case we have any money left.

There are six panels of red damask draperies, probably too large for our windows, but the fabric is good and they cost only $85. We'll have them and spend whatever it costs to remake them to fit. They should be far enough away to go with either the salmon pink ground or the yellow ground carpet.

KITTINGER & COMPANY, INC.

Sale ⚹64 had in it Lot 183, "a set of Louis XVI seat furniture consisting of three fauteuils with oval backs carved with ribbon cresting, padded arms and raised on turned fluted legs; together with a settee *en suite*. Each piece upholstered in an Aubusson tapestry woven with sprays of flowers on a pale green ground."

It sold for $650.

Although we haven't seen this suite of seat furniture, there are certain things about the catalogue description that stand out. To make one point, let's look at the description of Lot 181 "George III style Mahogany Sofa Table." And Lot 182—"Louis XV Style Ormolu mantle clock." But Lot 183 said, "Set of Louis XVI Seat Furniture." See the point? No mention of "Style" in the description of Lot 183. Just a straight statement, "Set of Louis XVI Seat Furniture."

WOOD AND HOGAN, INC.

*Above are fine contemporary reproductions made in England
by Wood and Hogan, in mahogany, the armchair priced at
$948 and the side chair at $690. As comparison, on facing page,
a similar set of eight Hepplewhite George III mahogany dining
chairs, dating from the last quarter of the eighteenth century,
were sold as a lot for $3,300. That's an average of $400 a chair.*

That does not mean that the set is eighteenth century, of the period of Louis XVI, made before the French Revolution which top-
pled him from his well-cushioned throne. What it probably means
is that it just might be eighteenth century, but is probably nineteenth century.

We know, too, from the description, that it is a well-made set.
The French were not in the habit of putting Aubusson tapestry on
just any piece of seat furniture.

Then why did it sell for only $650?

There may be any one of a dozen reasons. For one, a set of
Aubusson-covered seat furniture requires a certain formal setting.
It just wouldn't look right in a California stucco ranch, and that

rules out a big chunk of the potential buying audience at a Los Angeles auction.

For another, there would probably not be very much competition from dealers for that particular set, attractive though it may seem. In general, it can be assumed that outside the New York area, the number of dealers attending such auctions is much lower and the areas of their interest are likely to reflect the taste of the community in which they do business.

One thing I can say with some certainty. It was not just a freak price. There were also in the same sale Lot 201, a "Set of Louis XVI Style painted side chairs," at $325 and another set of six similar side chairs, Lot 202, at $400. And these were covered in cream velvet which would be far more acceptable in California than Aubusson tapestry.

There was another intriguing item in Sale ⚹64—Lot 221, a "Louis XVI Style Grand Bergère, the cartouche-shaped back with down-scrolled arms, shaped feet and raised on cabriole legs centering a shaped apron, the whole carved with scrolling acanthus

The new is not always more costly than the old. At right is a contemporary Pembroke table in mahogany by Kittinger, which can be bought for just under $500. Above, a comparable table in satinwood sold at Sotheby Parke Bernet for $1,800.

leaves; upholstered in Aubusson tapestry woven with flowers and an angel warming its hands at a fire."

It brought $150.

Whatever we decide about the Louis XVI set of three chairs and a settee upholstered in Aubusson at $650, let's keep that ber-

WOOD AND HOGAN, INC.

A George III style mahogany wine cooler, in a contemporary reproduction above, made in England by Wood and Hogan, Inc., is priced at $1,080. At right, a period piece made in the last quarter of the eighteenth century, the brass dimmed with age, sold for $850.

One of a pair of George III mahogany serpentine-fronted chests of drawers sold at Sotheby Parke Bernet for $3,000 the pair. By contrast, a fine contemporary reproduction made by Wood and Hogan in English workshops, on facing page, is priced at $3,330.

gère in mind as a possibility at $150. And we shouldn't overlook Lot 214, a "Pair of Louis XVI Style side chairs" painted with traces of gilding and upholstered in cream silk at $225, or Lot 220, a pair of Empire style painted and gilded fauteuils, upholstered in striped yellow velvet, at $200.

But before we settle on the suite of Louis XVI chairs, bargain though they may be at $650, let's see what else was offered. The only other settee or sofa in the sale was Lot 80, a Nineteenth Century Button Back Settee in the Egyptian Taste, at $80, a tempting price, but the mountings of bronze Egyptian masks make it definitely for a special taste and decor.

Sale #66, however, held a week later, offered a rich variety of sofas. There was Lot 108, an Empire-Style Mahogany Settee with classical ormolu mounts covered in green and cream linen, at $175, certainly an attractive buy. There was Lot 110, a Chinese Hardwood Three-Chair-Back Settee, a beautiful piece at $400, but it would require a seat pad and still would be less than cozy. Then there was Lot 122, a George III Style Mahogany Settee, upholstered, said the cataloguer with some disparagement, "in machine-woven tapestry," at $150. Then there was a Lot 136, a Chippendale Style Mahogany Sofa, with no indication of color in its covering, $150. And Lot 168, a Federal Style Mahogany Sofa, again no clue as to material or color, $175.

Here we are. The French furniture. Lot 289. "Louis XV Style Settee, the carved frame with a molded back rail of scrolling and shells, with down scrolled arms, the whole raised on cabriole legs; upholstered in floral linen." Or Lot 298, "mid-Nineteenth Century Style Button Back Settee, the scrolling molded frame carved with a floral cresting above an oval panel, with S-scroll arms, the whole raised on cabriole legs upholstered in pale rose velvet." $300.

That's about the choice. One unusual Chinese piece at $400 and several others ranging downward from $300. It can be assumed that those in which the description included the color and kind of fabric had coverings that were clean and serviceable, whereas the ones in which fabric was not mentioned probably needed to be recovered.

My own choice would be the nineteenth-century button back settee, Lot 298 at $300, the most expensive of the upholstered pieces. It would go equally well, in pale rose, with either the salmon rug or the yellow, which would be preferable. At this point, I think I would opt for the Chinese rug with its yellow ground and the Aubusson with its gray-green ground, since all together we have now spent only $300, plus $650 for the yellow ground rug, and $200 for the Aubusson carpet, plus $85 for the draperies, which must be recut and refitted. Total spent so far, $1,235. Now let's go back to the bergère, a nice piece by the fireplace (yes, our room has a fireplace, now that I think of it), at $150, and the two Empire-style side chairs, upholstered in striped yellow velvet, at $200. We'll stand them on the Aubusson rug, just so the yellows won't clash.

Now where are we? $1,235 plus $150 equals $1,385, plus $200 is $1,585. Just halfway into our budget. Now we need some cabinet-work and pictures and things to set on the mantel and tables. Not to mention lamps.

Let's look at English woods, if only because we already have a fair amount of carving on chair and sofa frames and the simple lines of Georgian will be a pleasant contrast.

Here's one. Just what we need in that corner over there. Lot 233 in the ⅞66 sale, a George III Style Mahogany dumbwaiter, formed of three graduating circular trays each supported by an urn-shaped pillar. Height 43 inches, $100. Three tiers to put things on. Great! And only $100! At today's prices the raw lumber would probably cost more.

This is a reading family, and Lot 187 is described as an Empire

Style Mahogany bookcase with a triangular pediment applied with an ormolu wreath tied with ribbons. Above are two glazed doors, and there are two drawers above two cupboard doors in the lower section. At $225, it would be just right for the setback to the right of the fireplace and the classical ormolu mounts will catch the glint of autumn fires there.

Georgian side tables are in short supply at these two sales, and we might have to wait until next month to find them. But if we're really pressed, there is an alternative. Chinese tables. There are three of them in Sale ⚡64, Lots 301 to 303, and a matching chair. Two are end tables 26 inches high, just right to stand next to the settee. One went for $70, the other for $30. The side chair went for $80 and a console table, 36 inches high, brought $100.

We were at $1,585 before the most recent purchases. Plus $100 for the dumbwaiter and $225 for the bookcase brings us to $1,910. And the Chinese wood pieces, $280 all together, $2,190. We still have roughly $800 for lamps, objects, and pictures. Lamps are also in short supply at these two sales, and it may be well to reserve a little money for a later sale. However, there is a pair of gilded wrought-iron and crystal sconces, each with two scrolling branches with lights hung with prisms and pear drops, 16 inches high, just right for above the fireplace, at $80, to flank a Regency overmantle mirror with a giltwood rectangular frame carved with paterae, lily leaves, and honeysuckle, $90.

And to stand on the mantel, I'm captured by a pair of English green parian-ware figures of young women, each wearing a loosely draped chiton (tunic). They are Minton, late nineteenth century, and brought $200. We will reserve decision on them until we see what we'll put on the dumbwaiter and on the walls. How about two framed watercolors by nineteenth-century Americans? One, by H. Peabody Flagg, a marine view of schooners under full sail off a rocky beach, $60. The other, by George Howell Gay, of a winter sunset landscape, $70. Both are framed. Or Lot 144, a seventeenth-century scene with two figures against a landscape, embroidered in crewelwork, $20. Or seven eighteenth-century Russian icons, which could be grouped on one wall, sold in two lots at Sale ⚡66, one for $60, the other for $80. Or prints. Five lithographs of Yvette Guilbert executed by D. Jamomet, of an unknown quality, after designs by Toulouse-Lautrec, all framed, in two lots, $40 and $30. Or Rouault woodcuts from the "*Reincarnations du Père Ubu*," three for $40, framed, numbered 73 of 305.

We could buy all the above, things and pictures, and still be under our $800. Or we could drop some and include others—an alabaster bust of Jeanne d'Arc, $90. Or an urn-shaped crystal vase, the shoulders with bacchanalian swags and grotesque masks, on an ormolu plinth, or subbase. Or a mid-eighteenth-century Bohemian ale glass mounted on a turned ivory base, $40.

But there is one piece in Sale ✕64 I would have found irresistible. The last item in the sale, Lot 317: "Late Eighteenth Century French Four Fold Screen, each rectangular panel applied with blockprinted paper depicting cherubs amid scrolling foliage and classical motifs, Height 5 feet 9 inches."

It sold for $10.

Does that make my point? Loud and clear? That you can furnish a living room and furnish it well, using reasonably good antiques and reasonably authentic works of art for under $3,000. Or for almost any amount you want to spend? Even $2,000. Or even less, if you bought only bottom-shelf bargains. At almost any group of sales, picked at random as these two catalogues were, almost anywhere in these United States where auctions are held.

Afterword

SINCE this project was launched, prices of art and antiques have peaked at levels that in many cases were probably above those cited in this volume. But from the summer of 1974, when both inflation and recession hit the market for Impressionist painters in London and Paris, there has been a substantial adjustment of prices all along the line.

Today, Impressionist pictures—the big expensive ones—have still shown no signs of recovery. And in general, market levels are back where they were when this book was begun. The most knowledgeable observers of the art auction market feel that the present "buyer's market" will continue for some time.

In any case, whatever the fluctuations of the economy around us, the market we are talking about continues to plod along, reacting much more slowly to general conditions than the more volatile market at the upper levels. It is safe to assume that today's inflated dollars, which will be with us for the foreseeable future, will prove an advantage to homemakers shopping the auctions, as long as prices remain behind the other wise general inflationary trend, as is still the case today.

HOWARD L. KATZANDER

Suggestions for Further Reading

THE AMERICAN IMPRESSIONISTS *by Donelson F. Hoopes.* 1972.
Watson-Guptill Publications, New York, N.Y.

AMERICAN PRIMITIVE PAINTING *by Jean Lipman.* 1972.
Dover Publications, Inc., New York, N.Y.

THE ANATOMY OF ANTIQUES *by Austin P. Kelley.* 1974.
The Viking Press, Inc., New York, N.Y.

THE APPEAL OF PRINTS *by Carl Zigrosser.* 1974.
Crown Publishers, Inc., New York, N.Y.

ART POTTERY OF THE U.S. *by Paul Evans.* 1974.
Charles Scribner's Sons, New York, N.Y.

CONNECTICUT CLOCKMAKERS *by Penrose R. Hoopes.* 1974.
Dover Publications, Inc., New York, N.Y.

FAKES *by Otto Kurz.* 1967.
Dover Publications, Inc., New York, N.Y.

FORGERIES, FAKES & REPRODUCTIONS *by George Savage.* 1970.
Praeger Publishers, Inc., New York, N.Y.

THE GENTLE ART OF FAKING FURNITURE *by Herbert Cescinsky.* 1967.
Dover Publications, Inc., New York, N.Y.

LETTERS OF THE GREAT ARTISTS, From Ghiberti to Pollack. 1963.
Random House, New York, N.Y.

LOOKING AT PICTURES *by Kenneth Clark.* 1968.
Beacon Press, New York, N.Y.
Author's Note: No better guide to the mysteries of fine art can be
found than Kenneth Clark, British art historian, as those who have
watched his television programs must know. These are some of his
other books:

CIVILIZATION: A Personal View. 1971.
Harper & Row, New York, N.Y.

LANDSCAPE INTO ART. 1976.
Harper & Row, New York, N.Y.

THE NUDE: A Study of Ideal Form. 1973.
Anchor Books, New York, N.Y.

REMBRANDT AND THE ITALIAN RENAISSANCE. 1968.
W. W. Norton & Company, Inc., New York, N.Y.

THE ROMANTIC REBELLION: Romantic vs. Classic Art. 1974.
Harper & Row, New York, N.Y.

MAINSTREAMS OF MODERN ART *by John Canaday.* 1959.
Holt, Rinehart & Winston, Inc., New York, N.Y.

OLD FURNITURE: Understanding the Craftsman's Art *by Nancy A. Smith.* 1975.
Bobbs-Merrill Co., Inc., New York, N.Y.

ORIENTAL CARPETS AND RUGS *by Stanley Reed.* 1972.
Crescent Books, New York, N.Y.

ORIENTAL RUGS, ANTIQUE & MODERN *by Walter A. Hawley.* 1970.
Dover Publications, Inc., New York, N.Y.

. . . *And for Reference*

AMERICAN GLASS PAPERWEIGHTS & THEIR MAKERS *by Jean S. Melvin.* 1967.
Nelson & Co., New York, N.Y.

THE BRITANNICA ENCYCLOPEDIA OF AMERICAN ART. 1973.
Simon & Schuster, Inc., New York, N.Y.

THE COMPLETE ENCYCLOPEDIA OF ANTIQUES *by L. G. G. Ramsey.* 1975.
Hawthorne Books, Inc., New York, N.Y.

THE COMPLETE GUIDE TO FURNITURE STYLES *by Louise A. Boger.* 1969.
Charles Scribner's Sons, New York, N.Y.

DICTIONARY OF ANTIQUES & DECORATIVE ARTS *by Louise Ade Boger and H. Batterson Boger.* 1971. Charles Scribner's Sons, New York, N.Y.

APPENDIX

Major Auction Houses

This list of auction houses in the United States gives some idea of the wide range of locations where auctions take place. While by no means the whole list, you can see that whether you live on the West Coast, in Tennessee, Maine, or somewhere in between, it is possible to take advantage of auctions in any part of the country.

ATLANTA AUCTION GALLERY 1405 Spring St. N.W., Atlanta, Georgia 30309

HARRIS AUCTION GALLERIES 875 N. Howard St., Baltimore, Maryland 21201

AMES ART GALLERIES 8729 Wilshire Blvd., Beverly Hills, California 90211

DAVID SHORE GALLERIES 415 Camden Drive, Beverly Hills, California 90210

JOSEPH LOUIS, INC. 840 Commonwealth Ave., Boston, Massachusetts 02115

DAVID BROTHERS AUCTION HOUSE 812 Elmwood Ave., Buffalo, New York 14222

TAIT AUCTION STUDIO 1209 Howard Ave., Burlingame, California 94010

CHICAGO ART GALLERIES, INC. 5960 N. Broadway, Chicago, Illinois 60626

HANZEL GALLERIES 1120 S. Michigan Ave., Chicago, Illinois 60605

SHERIDAN ART GALLERIES 4820 Sheridan Rd., Chicago, Illinois 60640

SHORE GALLERIES, INC. 3318 W. Devon Ave., Chicago, Illinois 60645

LOUIS ARONAFF 711 Sycamore St., Cincinnati, Ohio 45202

MAIN AUCTION CO. 137 W. 4th St., Cincinnati, Ohio 45202

FORDEM GALLERIES, INC. 3829 Lorain Ave., Cleveland, Ohio 44113

SAFRANS ANTIQUE GALLERIES 930 Gervais St., Columbia, South Carolina 29201

F. S. LONG & SONS 3126 E. 3rd St., Dayton, Ohio 45403

GARTH'S AUCTION BARN 1570 Stratford Rd., Delaware, Ohio 43015

DU MOUCHELLE ART GALLERY, INC. 409 E. Jefferson Ave., Detroit, Michigan 48226

ROBERT C. ELDRED East Dennis, Massachusetts 02641

O. RUNDLE GILBERT Garrison, New York 10524

M. LIPTON 18 S. Pauahi St., Honolulu, Hawaii 96813

PEYTON PLACE ANTIQUES 819 Lovett Blvd., Houston, Texas 77006

RICHARD A. BOURNE Box 141, Hyannis Port, Massachusetts 02647

MARVIN H. NEWMAN 426 S. Robertson Blvd., Los Angeles, California 90048

ERNEST RABOFF 849 N. La Cienga Blvd., Los Angeles, California 90069

SOTHEBY PARKE BERNET 7660 Beverly Blvd., Los Angeles, California 90036

D. V. CADY 2335 Frankfort Ave., Louisville, Kentucky 40206

JAMES, INC. 105 W. Main St., Louisville, Kentucky 40202

PALMER AUCTION SERVICE Lucas, Kansas 67648

MILWAUKEE AUCTION GALLERY 5466 N. Port Washington Rd., Milwaukee, Wisconsin 53217

WALL GALLERIES 724 N. Jefferson St., Milwaukee, Wisconsin 53202

COL. RAYMOND W. HUBER 211 N. Monroe, Montpelier, Ohio 43543

ARNETTE'S AUCTION GALLERY 310 Castle St., Murfreesboro, Tennessee 37130

AUCTION BARN R.F.D. ⚹2, New Milford, Connecticut 06776

FORSYTH-SANCHEZ AUCTION GALLERIES 1810 Magazine St., New Orleans, Louisiana 70130

LEVIN'S AUCTION EXCHANGE 414 Camp St., New Orleans, Louisiana 70130

MORTON'S AUCTION EXCHANGE 215 N. Rampart St., New Orleans, Louisiana 70112

ASTOR GALLERIES 754 N. Broadway, New York, New York 10003

CATHEDRAL AUCTION GALLERY 825 Broadway, New York, New York 10003

CHRISTIE, MANSON & WOODS 867 Madison Ave., New York, New York 10021

COLEMAN AUCTION GALLERY 525 E. 72nd St., New York, New York 10021

GRAMERCY AUCTION GALLERY 52 E. 13th St., New York, New York 10003

LAWNER'S AUCTIONS 81 University Place, New York, New York 10003

LUBIN GALLERIES, INC. 72 E. 13th St., New York, New York 10003

PLAZA ART & AUCTION GALLERY 406 E. 79th St., New York, New York 10021

SOTHEBY PARKE BERNET 980 Madison Ave., New York, New York 10021

TEPPER GALLERIES, INC. 3 W. 61st St., New York, New York 10023

VICTORIA GALLERY 106 Greenwich Ave., New York, New York 10010

EDDIE SEIGEL 242 W. 21st St., Norfolk, Virginia 23517

LAKESHORE AUCTION GALLERY 3000 Lakeside Ave., Oakland, California 94610

COQUINA AUCTION BARN 40 S. Atlantic Ave., Ormond Beach, Florida 32074

TROSBY, INC. 211 Royal Poinciana Way, Palm Beach, Florida 33480

CURTIS GALLERY 33 S. Raymond Ave., Pasadena, California 91101

S. T. FREEMAN & Co. 1818 Chestnut St., Philadelphia, Pennsylvania 19103

McPHERSON 4300 E. River Drive, Philadelphia, Pennsylvania 19129

HICKS AUCTIONS 4302 Oakwood Drive, Pleasant Hill, Iowa 48053

CHARLES GALLERIES, INC. 825 Woodward Ave., Pontiac, Michigan 48053

F. C. BAILEY Co. Free & South Streets, Portland, Maine 04111

FREDERICK BAILEY, INC. 383 Park Ave., Rochester, New York 14607

B. J. SELKIRK & SONS 4166 Olive St., St. Louis, Missouri 63108

BUTTERFIELD & BUTTERFIELD 1244 Sutter St., San Francisco, California 94108

GREENFIELD'S AUCTION MARKET 2001 2nd Ave., Seattle, Washington 98121

ROBERT LANDRY 94 Main St., South Essex, Massachusetts 01981

GEORGE'S AUCTION ROOMS 83 Summit Ave., Summit, New Jersey 07901

SUMMIT AUCTION ROOMS 47–49 Summit Ave., Summit, New Jersey 07901

C. G. SLOAN & Co. 715 13th St. N.W., Washington, D.C. 20005

ADAM A. WESCHLER & SON 905 E St. N.W., Washington, D.C. 20004

SCHMIDT'S 5138 W. Michigan Ave., Ypsilanti, Michigan 48197

An antique in need of repair or restoration can be a very sound purchase, as the text has shown. This list of selected restorers covers the range from furniture to glass, clocks, and carpets. If you have a painting you wish to restore, consult a nearby print shop, gallery, or if possible a college art department or museum for the names of qualified restorers.

ANTIQUES

ACADEMY LAMPS 517 N. Robertson Blvd., Los Angeles, California 90048

ROBERT CHEVOLOT 8687 Melrose Ave., Los Angeles, California 90069

HENRY K. CORDIER 1619 S. La Cienga Blvd., Los Angeles, California 90035

JOSEPH YOUNG 8422 Melrose Ave., Los Angeles, California 90069

MONTGOMERY ANTIQUES 140 W. Main St., Los Gatos, California 95030

V. J. LOVELL 2121 21st St. and 2114 P St., Sacramento, California 95814

WILLIAM ROBERT HASLET 5271 Linda Vista Rd., San Diego, California 92109

BRONSON TUFTS ANTIQUES 1572 Union St., San Francisco, California 94123

K. H. LENGFELD, INC. 1409 Sutter St., San Francisco, California 94109

ST. JOHN ANTIQUES 1612 Union St., San Francisco, California 94123

THOMAS UTLEY & ASSOC. 1842 Filmore St., San Francisco, California 94115

DAVID ESSINGTON 15 Calle Palo Colorado, Santa Barbara, California 93105

J. C. LAMB 3700 Franklin St., Denver, Colorado 80205

WINICK GALLERIES 4242 N.E. 2nd Ave., Miami, Florida 33138
ARNOLD'S ART CENTER 1712 E. 7th Ave., Tampa, Florida 33605
ANTHONY CERMAK 2406 Ballast Point Blvd., Tampa, Florida 33611

ART METAL PLATERS 6743 N. Clark St., Chicago, Illinois 60626
E. VINCENT DI SALVO & Co. 55 E. Washington St. Chicago, Illinois 60602
ALBERT HIGGINS 1423 N. Clark St., Chicago, Illinois 60610
KAKURO MATSUMOTO 226 S. Wabash Ave., Chicago, Illinois 60604

TAKOS & Co. 372 Main St., Dubuque, Iowa 52001

CARL G. PETERSON 6914 Highway, 69 Overland Park, Shawnee Mission, Kansas 66204

F. O. BAILEY Co. Free & South Streets, Portland, Maine 04111

ACE FURNITURE Co., INC. 2004 Maryland Ave., Baltimore, Maryland 21218
ADE FURNITURE 870 Linden Ave., Baltimore, Maryland 21201
CHIMNEY CORNER ANTIQUE SHOP St. Paul & Centre Streets, Baltimore, Maryland 21202
GROSSMAN & Co. 329 N. Charles St., Baltimore, Maryland 21201
ELISABETH C. G. PACKARD c/o WALTERS ART GALLERY 600 N. Charles St., Baltimore, Maryland 20201

GEBELEIN SILVERSMITHS, INC. 286 Newbury St., Boston, Massachusetts 02115
RED BRICK SCHOOLHOUSE Routes 5 & 10, Whately, Massachusetts 01093

AAAA ANTIQUE SHOP 2731 W. Grand Blvd., Detroit, Michigan 48208
DECOR ANTIQUES 16527 Hamilton Ave., Highland Park, Detroit, Michigan 48203
CENTURY HOUSE ANTIQUES 16527 Grand River St., Detroit, Michigan 48227
ROBERT CRAIGIE CABINET SHOP 15106 Kercheval Ave., Grosse Pointe, Michigan 48236

ALLEN'S ANTIQUE SHOP 8102 Evanston Ave., Raytown, Kansas City, Missouri 64138

OXFORD ANTIQUE RESTORERS, LTD. 37–20 48th Ave., Long Island City, New York 11100

VELEBA & HRUBAN 27–11 24th Ave., Astoria, New York 11103

ROBERT JENSEN, American Furniture, 23 Buckram Rd., Locust Valley, New York

CHALIKIAN JEWELERS, Clocks, watches, automatons, 103 Audrey Ave., Oyster Bay, New York 11771

RICHARDSON'S 511 Lawton St., New Rochelle, New York 10800

BENE DECORATORS 269 W. 231st St., Bronx, New York 10463

HARRY MARK 749 Fulton St., Brooklyn, New York 11217

SKYPE'S GALLERY 140 N. Broadway, Schenectady, New York 12305

THE JELLET STUDIO Glen Road, Southold, New York 11971

NATIONAL PLATING CO. 1501 Brewerton Rd., Syracuse, New York 13208

SAMUEL VITA 2704 Lodi St., Syracuse, New York 13208

ALEXANDER'S SCULPTURAL SERVICE, 117 E. 39th St., New York, N.Y. 10016

AMERICA SHOP, 319 E. 64th St., New York, N.Y. 10021

ARUNY & CO., 117 E. 29th St., New York, N.Y. 10016

MICHAEL BRUNO, 241 E. 127th St., New York, N.Y. 10035

CENTER ART STUDIO, 149 W. 57th St., New York, N.Y. 10019

COLLECK OF LONDON, 122 E. 58th St., New York, N.Y. 10022

CHARLES DEACON & SON, LTD., 353 E. 58th St., New York, N.Y. 10022

MICHAEL J. DOTZEL, 402 E. 63rd St., New York, N.Y. 10012

EMPIRE GLASS DECORATING CO., 262 Mott St., New York, N.Y. 10012

DAVID FARSANG, 1200 Lexington Ave., New York, N.Y. 10028

BENJAMIN FERBER, 351 E. 54th St., New York, N.Y. 10022

FIXIT MASTER, 937 Madison Ave., New York, N.Y. 10021

HARRY FUCHS, 715 Lexington Ave., New York, N.Y. 10022

GINSBURG & LEVY, INC., 815 Madison Ave., New York, N.Y. 10021

CHARLES R. GRACIE & SONS, 979 Third Ave., New York, N.Y. 10022

L. GRIEVE, INC., 972 Lexington Ave., New York, N.Y. 10021

HERTEL SILVER CO., 836 Broadway, New York, N.Y. 10003

HESS REPAIRS, 163 E. 33rd St., New York, N.Y. 10016

S. H. HOO, 680 Madison Ave., New York, N.Y. 10021

House of Screens, 219 E. 89th St., New York, N.Y. 10028
John Hunter Jones, 383 Third Ave., New York, N.Y. 10016
A. Kessler & Son, 207 Grand St., New York, N.Y. 10013
Ernest LoNano, 201 E. 67th St., New York, N.Y. 10021
Max's Art Metal Work, 165 Allen St., New York, N.Y. 10002
D. Miller, 166 E. 124th St., New York, N.Y. 10035
Old Antique Shop, 707 Lexington Ave., New York, N.Y. 10022
Florian Papp, Inc., 962 Madison Ave., New York, N.Y. 10021
James Patrick, 751 6th Ave., New York, N.Y. 10010
Gilbert Pelham, 986 Third Ave., New York, N.Y. 10022
John Russell, 255 E. 72nd St., New York, N.Y. 10021
Sigmund Rothschild, 27 W. 67th St., New York, N.Y. 10023
John H. Russell, 874 Lexington Ave., New York, N.Y. 10021
Sano Studio, 767 Lexington Ave., New York, N.Y. 10021
Max Schneider & Son, 175 E. 87th St., New York, N.Y. 10028
Charles Sandquist, Inc., 319 E. 53rd St., New York, N.Y. 10022
Thorp Bros., 315 E. 62nd St., New York, N.Y. 10021
Joseph Trighani & Son, 307 E. 53rd St., New York, N.Y. 10022
Frederick P. Victoria, 154 E. 55th St., New York, N.Y. 10022
Village Antique Repair Shop, 237 W. 13th St., New York, N.Y.
    10001
Piero Yengo, 340 E. 58th St., New York, N.Y. 10022
Zadina Metalcraft, 400 E. 66th St., New York, N.Y. 10021
Cherry Lane Enterprises, 64 Churchill St., Buffalo, New York
    14716
J. C. Dierdorf, 332 Esser Ave., Buffalo, New York 14207
Marsh Plating Co., 9 Carlton St., Buffalo, New York 14203
Carrie M. Rapp, 850 Broadway, Buffalo, New York 14212
Tripp Plating Works, Inc., 1491 William St., Buffalo, New York
    14206
J. Worfel & Sons, 934 Oak St., Syracuse, New York 13208
Roman Arts, Inc., 904 Nassau Road, Uniondale, New York 11553

Old Chapel Antique Shop, 3912 Eastern Ave., Cincinnati, Ohio
    45226

Harry Connelly, 1938 N. Portland Blvd., Portland, Oregon
    97217
Lamplighters, 2937 E. Burnside St., Portland, Oregon 97215
Fred Siedow 5744 E. Burnside St., Portland, Oregon 97215
C. A. Westervelt, 1931 S.E. Morrison St., Portland, Oregon
    97214

HERBERT SCHIFFER, INC., 609 W. Lancaster Pike, Exton, Pennsylvania 19341

ANTIQUE PLATING CO., 318 W. 18th St., Houston, Texas 77008
ROSE BEHAR, 2404 University Blvd., Houston, Texas 77005

JOHN WEIR, 1200 S. Alfred St., Alexandria, Virginia 22314
SHERMAN GALLERIES, 2910 Washington Ave., Newport News, Virginia 23607
HARMON HOUSE, 1909 Colonial Ave., Norfolk, Virginia 23517
MONTICELLO ANTIQUE SHOP, 227 W. York St., Norfolk, Virginia 23510
RHODES ANTIQUES, 514 Massachusetts Ave., Norfolk, Virginia 23508

ADAMS, DAVIDSON & CO., INC., 2322 P Street N.W., Washington, D.C. 20007
ANTIQUE MART, 4115 Wisconsin Ave. N.W., Washington, D.C. 20016
D. L. BRONWELL, INC., 710 12th St., Washington, D.C. 20002
CARLOS ANTIQUE SHOP, 8th & Columbia Rd., Washington, D.C. 20009
FRENCH SHOP, 631 Wisconsin Ave. N.W., Washington, D.C. 20007
HOFFMAN'S, 2447 18th St. N.W., Washington, D.C. 20009
HARRY C. JOHNSON & SON, 2110 5th St. N.W., Washington, D.C. 20002
KRUPSAW'S, 1420 Wisconsin Ave. N.W., Washington, D.C. 20007
MARIO'S ART SHOP, 2405 18th St. N.W., Washington, D.C. 20009
JAMES MOSS, 5840 McArthur Blvd. N.W., Washington, D.C. 20016
NONOMURA STUDIOS, 3432 Connecticut Ave. N.W., Washington, D.C. 20008
ORIENTAL ARTS SHOPS, 1620 Wisconsin Ave. N.W., Washington, D.C. 20007

FURNITURE

WILLIAM ROBERT HASLET, 5271 Linda Vista Rd., San Diego, California 92109
K. H. LENGFELD, INC., 1409 Sutter St., San Francisco, California 94109

L. L. DENSMORE, 120 W. Gutierrez St., Santa Barbara, California 93101

RIKKI'S STUDIOS, INC., 2556 Corack Way, Miami, Florida 33134

E. R. WILKERSON, 3300 Peidmont Rd. N.E., Atlanta, Georgia 30305

L. L. BONNECARRERE, 1616 Orleans Ave., New Orleans, Louisiana 70116
HOLTZENDORF'S FURNITURE FINISHING, 1430 Terpichore St., New Orleans, Louisiana 70301

MAURICE E. REID, 8470 Perry Rd., Atlas, Michigan 48411

ANTIQUE FURNITURE RESTORERS CORP., 225 E. 24th St., New York, N.Y. 10010
B. BASSO, 434 E. 72nd St., New York, N.Y. 10021
BRESSLER FURNITURE REPAIRING CO., 1268 St. Nicholas Ave., New York, N.Y. 10033
COLLECK OF LONDON, 122 E. 57th St., New York, N.Y. 10022
CHARLES DEACON & SONS, INC., 353 E. 58th St., New York, N.Y. 10022
HEDE FISCHER-PLATHEN, 405 E. 72nd St., New York, N.Y. 10021
FRENCH & ENGLISH FURNITURE CO., INC., 427 E. 76th St., New York, N.Y. 10021
CHARLES R. GRACIE & SONS, 979 Third Ave., New York, N.Y. 10022
SIGMUND ROTHSCHILD, 27 W. 67th St., New York, N.Y. 10023
ISRAEL SACK, 15 E. 57th St., New York, N.Y. 10022
SARASI FURNITURE CORP., 223 E. 80th St., New York, N.Y. 10021
SUBACCHI, 650 First Ave., New York, N.Y. 10016
THINGS ANTIQUE, INC., 250 W. 77th St., New York, N.Y. 10024
COMFORT FURNITURE CO., 1310 Broadway, Buffalo, New York 14212
HARRY MARK, 749 Fulton St., Brooklyn, New York 11217
SKYPE'S GALLERY, 140 N. Broadway, Schenectady, New York 12305
J. WORFEL & SONS, 934 Oak St., Syracuse, New York 13208

JASTROMB ART FURNITURE, INC., 46 Ravena, Hudson, Ohio 44236

DORIS & BILL JACKSON, Culver Drive S.E., Salem, Oregon 97301

RUDOLPH, INC., 1311 West Chester Park, West Chester, Pennsylvania 19380

JAMES E. SCUDDER, Route 112, Carolina, Rhode Island 02812

AAA FURNITURE REFINISHING, 2432 Savannah Highway, Charleston, South Carolina 29407

WISHNOW FURNITURE & ANTIQUES, 2301 Waugh Drive, Houston, Texas 77006

C. N. HURET, 3288 M St. N.W., Washington D.C. 20007
LAUNAY & CO., INC., 2410 18th St. N.W., Washington, D.C. 20009

RUGS / CARPETS

MARK KESHISHIAN & SONS, INC., 6930 Wisconsin Ave. N.W., Washington, D.C. 20015

NAHIGAN BROTHERS, INC., 737 N. Michigan Ave., Chicago, Illinois 60611

MUSA EID MUSA, 1246 Perkomen Ave., Reading, Pennsylvania 19602

GLASS / PORCELAIN

GLASS & PORCELAIN
BETTY ROBERTS, 94–82 N. Canon Drive, Beverly Hills, California 90210

HARRY BURKE, 1801 Chestnut St., Philadelphia, Pennsylvania 19103

GLASS
GLASSART STUDIO, 7121 5th Ave., Scottsdale, Arizona 85251

L. L. BONNECARRERE, 1616 Orleans Ave., New Orleans, Louisiana 70116

PORCELAIN

HARRY EBERHARDT & SON, 2010 Walnut St., Philadelphia, Pennsylvania 19103

A. L. KLEIN & SON, 621 S. 9th St., Philadelphia, Pennsylvania 19147

CLOCKS

CALICO CAT ANTIQUES, P. O. Box 758, Evergreen, Colorado 80439

LIEBMAN CLOCK COMPANY, 356 N.E. 167th St., Miami, Florida 33162

LAURELWOOD ANTIQUES, Laurelwood Drive, Ashby, Massachusetts 01431

CENTURY HOUSE ANTIQUES, 17740 Grand River St., Detroit, Michigan 48227

MICHIGAN ANTIQUE SHOP, 2124 Michigan Ave., Detroit, Michigan 48216

THE ANTIQUE NOOK, P. O. Box 338, 6226 Waterloo St., Atwater, Ohio 44201

OLD COUNTRY WATCHMAKER, 10110 Main St., Bellevue, Washington 98004

SILVER

H. H. GAUVIN, 1122 4th Ave., San Diego, California 92101

DICK VAN ERP, 773 14th St., San Francisco, California 94114

CURRIER & ROBY, 40 W. 17th St., New York, N.Y. 10011

HERTEL SILVER COMPANY, 836 Broadway, New York, N.Y. 10003

VILLAGE SILVERSMITHS, 3405 Putnam Place, Bronx, New York 10467

ROBERT ROGERS, 2170 Wantagh Park Drive, Wantagh, New York 11793

J. DE VOREN, 6350 Germantown Ave., Philadelphia, Pennsylvania 19103

KLEIN JEWELRY, 1009 E St. N.W., Washington, D.C. 20004
ARPAD & HENRY, INC., 3125 M St., Washington, D.C. 20007

TAPESTRIES

BESHAR & CO., INC., 63 E. 52nd St., New York, N.Y. 10022
CHAMALIAN, 785 Madison Ave., New York, N.Y. 10021
H. CHAMALIAN & SON, 305 E. 63rd St., New York, N.Y. 10021
DILDRIAN, INC., 762 Madison Ave., New York, N.Y. 10021

LAMPS

LAMP POST ANTIQUES, 3055 Riverside Ave., Jacksonville, Florida 32205

LORENE'S ANTIQUE LAMPS, 1000 N. York St., Dearborn, Michigan 48128

LEEDELL E. REESE, 1559 Magazine St., New Orleans, Louisiana 70130

BAROMETERS/MIRRORS

ALDEN STUDIOS, INC., 1030 Louisiana Ave., New Orleans, Louisiana 70115

GILTS

WALTERS GALLERY, Main St., Woodbury, Connecticut 06798

CHINA

VAN PARYS STUDIO, 6338 Germantown Ave., Philadelphia, Pennsylvania 19144

CURIOSITY SHOP, Box 73, Sedan, Kansas 67361

SCULPTURE

RENATO LUCCHETTI, 537 N. Oxford St., Arlington, Virginia 22203

PRINTS (*drawings*)

EMERSON GALLERY, 17230 Ventura Blvd., Encino, California 91316
GRAPHICS GALLERY, 1 Embarcardero Center, San Francisco, California 94111

HOLMAN'S PRINT SHOP, 28 Court Square Boston, Massachusetts 02108

JEWELRY

JOHN COOK, 647 Broadway, San Diego, California 92101

American Primitive Painters

Here is a list of primitive painters who were active in the northeastern sector of the United States mainly during the nineteenth century. The names are followed by the locale where they are known to have worked and the date or dates when they flourished, taken from known paintings by their hand.

ARTIST	LOCALE	DATE
James Bard	—	1850
Lucius Barnes	Middletown, Connecticut	1810–30
Lucy Bartlett	Massachusetts	1830
William T. Bartol	Marblehead, Massachusetts	1845
Ruth Henshaw Bascom	Massachusetts	1772–1830
O. I. Bears	New London, Connecticut	1835
Zedekiah Belknap	Massachusetts	1810–40
Alexandre Boudrou	Pennsylvania	1850
John Brewster	Portland, Maine	1830
H. Bundy	Claremont, New Hampshire	1837–50
Hannah P. Buxton	New York	1820
Joseph Goodhue Chandler	Boston, Massachusetts	1840
Winthrop Chandler	Massachusetts	1749–90
Eleanor L. Coward	—	—
Mary Cushman	Rhode Island	1800
J. Dalee	Cambridge, New York	1830
Eben Davis	Massachusetts	1850
E. P. Davis	Massachusetts	1820
Polly C. Dean	Massachusetts	1820
Erastus Salisbury Field	Massachusetts	1805–1900
E. E. Finch	Maine	1850
J. C. Goodell	Malden Bridge, New York	1830

Benjamin Greenleaf	Phippsburg, Maine	1820–40
Dr. Rufus Hathaway	Massachusetts	1790
Matilda A. Haviland	—	—
Edward Hicks	Bucks County, Pennsylvania	1780–1849
William Hillyer	New Jersey	1830
Mary L. Ingraham	Massachusetts	1810
Ann Johnson	Connecticut	1810–25
John Johnston	York, Maine	1790
Charles King	Maine	1850
Betsy B. Lathrop	New York	1810
Reuben Moulthrop	Massachusetts	1790
Edward Plummer	Connecticut	1850
William Mathew Prior	Massachusetts	1806–73
S. Rosen	Williamsport, Pennsylvania	1860–70
Joseph Whitney Stock	Springfield, Massachusetts	1815–55
Cephas Thompson	Bath, Maine	1835
Catherine Townsend Warner	Rhode Island	1810
Susan Whitcomb	Brandon, Vermont	1840
Matilda Wilder	Massachusetts	1820
John Wilkie	—	1840
Micah Williams	Peekskill, New York	1790
Mary R. Wilson	Massachusetts	1820

Note: There were hundreds of other primitive painters who flourished in the late eighteenth and through the nineteenth centuries. Those listed here are among the painters whose work turns up frequently in the areas indicated.

INDEX